Spelling Workbook

CONCORDIA COLLEGE LIBRARY
BRONXVILLE, NY 10708

Scott Foresman

Editorial Offices: Glenview, Illinois • Parsippany, New Jersey • New York, New York
Sales Offices: Reading, Massachusetts • Duluth, Georgia • Glenview, Illinois
Carrollton, Texas • Ontario, California

Copyright © Scott Foresman, a division of Addison-Wesley
Educational Publishers, Inc. All Rights Reserved. Printed in the United
States of America. This publication is protected by Copyright and
permission should be obtained from the publisher prior to any prohibited
reproduction, storage in a retrieval system, or transmission in any form
or by any means, electronic, mechanical, photocopying, recording, or
likewise. For information regarding permission(s), write to: Permissions
Department, Scott Foresman, 1900 East Lake Avenue, Glenview, Illinois
60025.

Editorial Offices
Glenview, Illinois • Parsippany, New Jersey • New York, New York

Sales Offices
Reading, Massachusetts • Duluth, Georgia • Glenview, Illinois
Carrollton, Texas • Ontario, California

ISBN 0-328-01654-3

11-PRO-06 05 04

Table of Contents

Unit 1

Discovering Ourselves

	Pretest	Think and Practice	Proofread and Write	Review
Tony and the Snark Short Vowels	1	2	3	4
Teammates Words with *ei* and *ie*	5	6	7	8
April's Mud Vowel Sounds in *rule* and *view*	9	10	11	12
Hot Dogs and Bamboo Shoots Vowel Sounds with *r*	13	14	15	16
The Telephone Call Getting Letters in Correct Order	17	18	19	20

Unit 2

The Living Earth

	Pretest	Think and Practice	Proofread and Write	Review
A Trouble-Making Crow Words from Many Cultures	21	22	23	24
From a Spark Unexpected Consonant Spellings	25	26	27	28
Storm-a-Dust Compound Words 1	29	30	31	32
The Day of the Turtle Compound Words 2	33	34	35	36
Saving the Sound Words with No Sound Clues	37	38	39	40

Unit 3

Goals Great and Small

	Pretest	Think and Practice	Proofread and Write	Review
Elizabeth Blackwell: Medical Pioneer Suffixes -ance, -ence, -ant, -ent	41	42	43	44
Born Worker Irregular Plurals	45	46	47	48
Wilma Unlimited Vowels in Unstressed Syllables	49	50	51	52
Casey at the Bat Vowels in Final Syllables	53	54	55	56
The Night of the Pomegranate Homophones	57	58	59	60

Unit 4

The Way We Were—The Way We Are

	Pretest	Think and Practice	Proofread and Write	Review
Spring Paint Using Just Enough Letters	61	62	63	64
A Brother's Promise Including All the Letters	65	66	67	68
from **Catching the Fire** Adding -ed and -ing	69	70	71	72
The Seven Wonders of the Ancient World One Consonant or Two?	73	74	75	76
The Gold Coin Related Words I	77	78	79	80

Unit 5

Into the Unknown

	Pretest	Think and Practice	Proofread and Write	Review
To the Pole Negative Prefixes	81	82	83	84
***from* El Güero** Suffixes *-ation, -tion, -ion*	85	86	87	88
Destination: Mars Opposite Prefixes	89	90	91	92
The Land of Expectations Suffixes *-ate, -ive, -ship*	93	94	95	96
The Trail Drive Using Apostrophes	97	98	99	100

Unit 6

I've Got It!

	Pretest	Think and Practice	Proofread and Write	Review
Noah Writes a B & B Letter Easily Confused Words	101	102	103	104
Louis Braille Vowel Sounds /oi/, /ou/, /ȯ/	105	106	107	108
The Librarian Who Measured the Earth Words from Greek and Latin	109	110	111	112
Tyree's Song Words with *ci* and *ti*	113	114	115	116
Cutters, Carvers, and the Cathedral Related Words 2	117	118	119	120

Tony and the Snark

Spelling: Short Vowels

Pretest Directions: Fold back the page along the dotted line. On the blanks, write the spelling words as they are dictated. When you have finished the test, unfold the page and check your words.

1. _____	1. We **admire** beautiful sunsets.
2. _____	2. The **canyon** was very deep.
3. _____	3. Use a microscope to **magnify** it.
4. _____	4. The old ship has a **cannon**.
5. _____	5. Offer him a glass of **lemonade**.
6. _____	6. What new **method** did you use?
7. _____	7. The bakers **decorate** the cake.
8. _____	8. She ran the longest **distance**.
9. _____	9. Let's go **swimming** tomorrow.
10. _____	10. His parents are not very **strict**.
11. _____	11. Her **injury** was not too serious.
12. _____	12. I need a **tissue**.
13. _____	13. My sister studies **modern** dance.
14. _____	14. This movie is a **comedy**.
15. _____	15. He is known for his **honesty**.
16. _____	16. This land is private **property**.
17. _____	17. Her **husband** gave her a ring.
18. _____	18. I get **clumsy** when I am tired.
19. _____	19. The **hundredth** customer wins.
20. _____	20. The castle has an old **dungeon**.

Pretest

Notes for Home: Your child took a pretest on words that have short vowel sounds. *Home Activity:* Help your child learn misspelled words before the final test. Your child should look at the word, say it, spell it aloud, and then spell it with eyes shut.

Spelling: Short Vowels 1

Name_____   Tony and the Snark

Spelling: Short Vowels

Word List			
admire	method	injury	property
canyon	decorate	tissue	husband
magnify	distance	modern	clumsy
cannon	swimming	comedy	hundredth
lemonade	strict	honesty	dungeon

Directions: Choose the words from the box that have a short **u, a,** or **i** vowel sound. Write each word in the correct column.

Short u as in under

1. _____
2. _____
3. _____
4. _____

Short a as in land

5. _____
6. _____
7. _____
8. _____

Short i as in fit

9. _____
10. _____
11. _____
12. _____
13. _____

Directions: Choose the word from the box that contains each word below. Write the word on the line.

_____ 14. rate
_____ 15. prop
_____ 16. mode
_____ 17. lemon
_____ 18. one
_____ 19. met
_____ 20. come

Notes for Home: Your child spelled words with short vowel sounds: *a* as in *apple*, *e* as in *leg*, *i* as in *tin*, *o* as in *concert*, *u* as in *hunt*. **Home Activity:** Write each word on a slip of paper. Take turns choosing a word and using it in a sentence.

2 Spelling: Short Vowels

Name _____   Tony and the Snark

Spelling: Short Vowels

Directions: Proofread this diary entry. Find five spelling mistakes. Use the proofreading marks to correct each mistake.

≡ Make a capital.
/ Make a small letter.
∧ Add something.
⌒ Take out something.
⊙ Add a period.
¶ Begin a new paragraph.

August 19th

This is my first time sailing at night. The dark seems to magnfy each sound. I can hear the surf in the distence booming like a canon. I think I like sailing at night because I can lie on deck and admire the stars, which decarate the sky like so many tiny lights.

I'd better get some sleep. Tomorrow we are sailing to our friend's beach property to go swiming at her house.

Proofread and Write

Spelling Tip

swimming
Remember to double the final consonant of one-syllable words that end with **consonant-vowel-consonant.**

Word List

admire	method	injury	property
canyon	decorate	tissue	husband
magnify	distance	modern	clumsy
cannon	swimming	comedy	hundredth
lemonade	strict	honesty	dungeon

Write a Diary Entry

Imagine you are the captain of a large ship. On a separate sheet of paper, write a diary entry from the captain's personal log. Try to use at least five of your spelling words.

Notes for Home: Your child spelled words with short vowel sounds: *a* as in *apple*, *e* as in *leg*, *i* as in *tin*, *o* as in *concert*, *u* as in *hunt*. **Home Activity:** Have your child demonstrate the difference between a short *e* sound and a long *e* sound, using a variety of words.

Spelling: Short Vowels

Name _____   Tony and the Snark

Spelling: Short Vowels   REVIEW

Word List

admire	lemonade	swimming	modern	husband
canyon	method	strict	comedy	clumsy
magnify	decorate	injury	honesty	hundredth
cannon	distance	tissue	property	dungeon

Directions: Choose the word from the box that best completes each sentence. Write the word on the line to the left.

_____ 1. My favorite drink on a hot day is _____.

_____ 2. My brother-in-law is my sister's _____.

_____ 3. A bicycle helmet may protect you from an _____.

_____ 4. Every Fourth of July, a ball is fired from the old _____.

_____ 5. Wendy and I are on our way to the lake to go _____.

_____ 6. The jail in a castle is called a _____.

_____ 7. We laughed and laughed at a television _____.

_____ 8. I am going to sneeze; please hand me a _____.

_____ 9. I called it a valley, but Sue said it is a _____.

_____ 10. One out of one hundred is one _____.

Directions: Choose the word from the box that has the same or nearly the same meaning as each word below. Write the word on the line.

11. possession _____   16. enlarge _____

12. truthfulness _____   17. way _____

13. rigid _____   18. length _____

14. adorn _____   19. current _____

15. respect _____   20. awkward _____

Notes for Home: Your child spelled words with short vowel sounds: *a* as in *apple*, *e* as in *leg*, *i* as in *tin*, *o* as in *concert*, *u* as in *hunt*. **Home Activity:** Scramble the letters of each spelling word. Have your child unscramble each word.

4 Spelling: Short Vowels

Name _____

Teammates

Spelling: Words with *ei* and *ie*

Pretest Directions: Fold back the page along the dotted line. On the blanks, write the spelling words as they are dictated. When you have finished the test, unfold the page and check your words.

1. _____
2. _____
3. _____
4. _____
5. _____
6. _____
7. _____
8. _____
9. _____
10. _____
11. _____
12. _____
13. _____
14. _____
15. _____
16. _____
17. _____
18. _____
19. _____
20. _____

1. There is a cobweb on the **ceiling**.
2. The cashier gave him a **receipt**.
3. I did not mean to **deceive** you.
4. **Neither** John nor Jamila will go.
5. You may do it at your **leisure**.
6. Many foods provide **protein**.
7. He is the team's wide **receiver**.
8. **Seize** the opportunity.
9. He is very **conceited**.
10. The cows graze in the **field**.
11. You can **achieve** your dreams.
12. That is a farfetched **belief**.
13. Let's keep this talk **brief**.
14. The rain was a welcome **relief**.
15. We made four dollars **apiece**.
16. The knight picks up his **shield**.
17. I am my aunt's only **niece**.
18. The truck runs on **diesel** fuel.
19. Accidents can cause **grief**.
20. Cars must **yield** to pedestrians.

Pretest

Notes for Home: Your child took a pretest on words with the letters *ei* and *ie*. **Home Activity:** Help your child learn misspelled words before the final test. Your child can underline the word parts that caused the problems and concentrate on those parts.

Spelling: Words with *ei* and *ie* 5

Name _____   Teammates

Spelling: Words with ei and ie

Word List

ceiling	leisure	conceited	brief	niece
receipt	protein	field	relief	diesel
deceive	receiver	achieve	apiece	grief
neither	seize	belief	shield	yield

Directions: Choose the words from the box that rhyme with each word below. Write the words on the lines.

wield
1. _____
2. _____
3. _____

piece
4. _____
5. _____

either
6. _____

thief
7. _____
8. _____
9. _____
10. _____

believe
11. _____
12. _____

Directions: Choose the word from the box that best completes each sentence. Write the word on the line to the left.

_____ 13. Luis's pride in his home runs made him seem _____ to some people.

_____ 14. However, Luis worked hard, practicing even during _____ time on days off.

_____ 15. The _____ from Mighty Mike's Batting Cages showed the number of hours Luis spent practicing.

_____ 16. Luis had to _____ the moment before they lost the game.

_____ 17. It was a good thing they played in an outdoor stadium, because the ball Luis hit would have broken any _____ overhead.

_____ 18. Luis ran around the bases as if on _____ fuel.

_____ 19. Luis was the proud _____ of his teammates' congratulations.

_____ 20. "It was the _____ in the hot dogs that did it!" Luis joked.

Notes for Home: Your child spelled words with *ei* and *ie*. **Home Activity:** Have your child name two words, one with *ei* and one with *ie*, that have the long *e* sound as in *believe*. Make sure your child can spell each word correctly.

6   Spelling: Words with *ei* and *ie*

Name _____

Teammates

Spelling: Words with *ei* and *ie*

Directions: Proofread this poem. Find five spelling mistakes. Use the proofreading marks to correct each mistake.

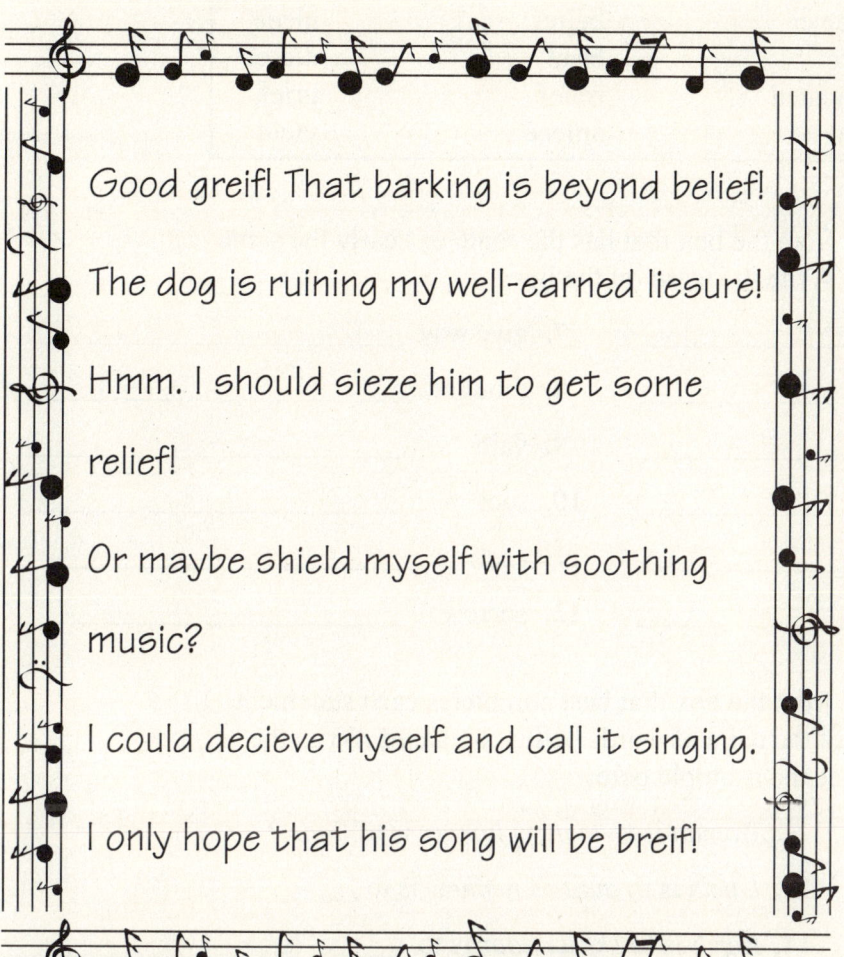

Good greif! That barking is beyond belief!

The dog is ruining my well-earned liesure!

Hmm. I should sieze him to get some relief!

Or maybe shield myself with soothing music?

I could decieve myself and call it singing.

I only hope that his song will be breif!

	Make a capital.
/	Make a small letter.
∧	Add something.
⍭	Take out something.
⊙	Add a period.
¶	Begin a new paragraph.

Spelling Tip

seize   diesel

It is easy to misspell words in which the long **e** sound is spelled **ei** or **ie**. Check the poem carefully to be sure the **ei** and **ie** words are spelled correctly.

Word List

ceiling	leisure	conceited	brief	niece
receipt	protein	field	relief	diesel
deceive	receiver	achieve	apiece	grief
neither	seize	belief	shield	yield

Write a Poem

On a separate sheet of paper, write a poem in which you describe how your tolerance was tested. How did you handle the situation? What did it teach you about being tolerant? Try to use at least three of your spelling words.

Notes for Home: Your child spelled words with *ei* and *ie*. **Home Activity:** Take turns saying and spelling each word from the box. Continue adding and practicing other hard-to-spell *ei* and *ie* words.

Spelling: Words with *ei* and *ie*   7

Name _____

Teammates

Spelling: Words with ei and ie

REVIEW

Word List			
ceiling	protein	achieve	shield
receipt	receiver	belief	niece
deceive	seize	brief	diesel
neither	conceited	relief	grief
leisure	field	apiece	yield

Directions: Choose the word from the box that has the same or nearly the same meaning as each word below. Write the word on the line.

1. sales slip _____
2. gain _____
3. comfort _____
4. lie _____
5. relaxation _____
6. grab _____
7. give way _____
8. thought _____
9. vain _____
10. fuel _____
11. each _____
12. sorrow _____

Directions: Choose the word from the box that best completes each statement. Think about the relationship of the pairs of words being compared. Write the word on the line to the left. See the example below.

Woman is to *man* as *lioness* is to *lion.*

_____ 13. *Uncle* is to *aunt* as *nephew* is to _____.

_____ 14. *Earth* is to *sky* as *floor* is to _____.

_____ 15. *Catcher* is to *mask* as *knight* is to _____.

_____ 16. *Pitcher* is to *catcher* as *sender* is to _____.

_____ 17. *Fish* is to *stream* as *sheep* is to _____.

_____ 18. *All* is to *none* as *both* is to _____.

_____ 19. *Spinach* is to *iron* as *meat* is to _____.

_____ 20. *Tall* is to *short* as *lasting* is to _____.

Notes for Home: Your child spelled words with *ei* and *ie*. **Home Activity:** Point out that if you can spell *belief,* you can spell *believe.* Then have your child name other words you can spell if you can spell *receipt, deceive,* and *relief* correctly.

8   Spelling: Words with *ei* and *ie*

Name_____

April's Mud

Spelling: Vowel Sounds in *rule* and *view*

Pretest Directions: Fold back the page along the dotted line. On the blanks, write the spelling words as they are dictated. When you have finished the test, unfold the page and check your words.

1. _____
2. _____
3. _____
4. _____
5. _____
6. _____
7. _____
8. _____
9. _____
10. _____
11. _____
12. _____
13. _____
14. _____
15. _____
16. _____
17. _____
18. _____
19. _____
20. _____

1. The store must **reduce** its staff.
2. She has a casual **attitude**.
3. It will be a **costume** party.
4. The night was **absolutely** dark.
5. I **assume** you know each other?
6. The **sewer** flooded in the storm.
7. They moved to **New York** City.
8. I must **renew** my membership.
9. Let us **review** today's lesson.
10. He has a detached **viewpoint**.
11. The reporters **interview** the star.
12. We went to a **preview** of the film.
13. Which cereal is the better **value**?
14. **Continue** with your game.
15. The **rescue** team arrived in time.
16. It's **humid** by the seashore.
17. The **universe** must be vast.
18. The soldier put on his **uniform**.
19. She went to her class **reunion**.
20. The **United States** is a country.

Pretest

Notes for Home: Your child took a pretest on words with vowel sounds such as those in *rule* and *view*. **Home Activity:** Help your child learn misspelled words before the final test. Dictate the word and have your child spell the word aloud for you or write it on paper.

Spelling: Vowel Sounds in *rule* and *view*

Name _____ April's Mud

Spelling: Vowel Sounds in *rule* and *view*

Word List

reduce	assume	review	value	United States
attitude	sewer	viewpoint	continue	universe
costume	New York	interview	rescue	uniform
absolutely	renew	preview	humid	reunion

Directions: Choose the words from the box that have the same vowel sound as **rule**. Write each word in the correct column.

Spelled u-consonant-e

1. _____
2. _____
3. _____
4. _____
5. _____

Spelled ew

6. _____
7. _____
8. _____

Directions: Choose the words from the box that have the same vowel sound as **view** spelled **iew**. Write the words on the lines.

9. _____   11. _____
10. _____   12. _____

Directions: Find eight words from the box in the puzzle. They may be printed across or down. Circle the words in the puzzle. Then write them on the lines. Hint: Each word has the same vowel sound as **view** spelled **ue** or **u**.

13. _____
14. _____
15. _____
16. _____
17. _____
18. _____
19. _____
20. _____

```
U N I T E D S T A T E S
N Y E X T A R W U R R O
I A W H U M I D N E E L
V A L U E O R E S C U E
E C O N T I N U E U N P
R C A S E B M E O C I Z
S H P M D D W S R E O I
E V U N I F O R M T N L
```

Notes for Home: Your child spelled words with the vowel sounds in *rule* (spelled *u-consonant-e* and *ew*) and *view* (spelled *iew, ue,* and *u*). **Home Activity:** Ask your child to name some words that rhyme with *view*. Discuss how each rhyming word is spelled.

Name _____ April's Mud

Spelling: Vowel Sounds in *rule* and *view*

Directions: Proofread this advertisement. Find five spelling mistakes. Use the proofreading marks to correct each mistake.

Proofreading Marks
≡ Make a capital.
/ Make a small letter.
∧ Add something.
ℐ Take out something.
⊙ Add a period.
¶ Begin a new paragraph.

Build Your Own Home!

Why live in a unifrom house like everyone else's?

Redeuce the expense of hiring builders!

Build it yourself!

A place you have built yourself will have far greater valiew than a place made for other people!

It's fun! It's easy! Read all about it!

Prevue, interview, and consultation absoluetly free!

Spelling Tip
New York   United States
Remember to capitalize both words in place names such as **New York** and **United States.**

Word List
reduce	interview
attitude	preview
costume	value
absolutely	continue
assume	rescue
sewer	humid
New York	United States
renew	universe
review	uniform
viewpoint	reunion

Write an Advertisement

On a separate sheet of paper, write an advertisement to sell a product of your choice. Try to use at least three of your spelling words.

Notes for Home: Your child spelled words with the vowel sounds in *rule* (spelled *u-consonant-e* and *ew*) and *view* (spelled *iew, ue,* and *u*). **Home Activity:** Write each spelling word, deliberately misspelling some words. Have your child check and correct the words.

Spelling: Vowel Sounds in *rule* and *view*   11

Name_____   April's Mud

Spelling: Vowel Sounds in *rule* and *view*

REVIEW

Word List			
reduce	sewer	interview	humid
attitude	New York	preview	United States
costume	renew	value	universe
absolutely	review	continue	uniform
assume	viewpoint	rescue	reunion

Directions: Choose the word from the box that best completes each sentence. Write the word on the line to the left.

_____ 1. "The _____ is as much fun as Italy!" exclaimed Tony.

_____ 2. Here he did not have to wear a _____ to school.

_____ 3. From Tony's _____, his temporary new home looked good.

_____ 4. Tony visited the famous city of _____ in the fall.

_____ 5. He wore a fancy _____ to march in the San Genaro parade.

_____ 6. It was so crowded that it seemed as if everyone in the _____ must be there.

_____ 7. The _____ weather made Tony so warm he almost fainted.

_____ 8. Another marcher had to _____ Tony from being trampled.

_____ 9. Tony decided to _____ his layers of clothing to stay cooler.

_____ 10. Later, he sent his little sister a newspaper _____ of the parade.

Directions: Choose the word from the box that best matches each definition. Write the word on the line.

11. positively; certainly _____
12. talk with; question _____
13. a gathering after separation _____
14. a pipe for carrying waste _____
15. manner _____
16. make like new; restore _____
17. view or show in advance _____
18. take for granted _____
19. keep on; not stop _____
20. worth or importance _____

Notes for Home: Your child spelled words with the vowel sounds in *rule* (spelled *u-consonant-e* and *ew*) and *view* (spelled *iew, ue,* and *u*). **Home Activity:** Help your child use the spelling words in sentences.

12 Spelling: Vowel Sounds in *rule* and *view*

Name_____ Hot Dogs and Bamboo Shoots

Spelling: Vowel Sounds with *r*

Pretest Directions: Fold back the page along the dotted line. On the blanks, write the spelling words as they are dictated. When you have finished the test, unfold the page and check your words.

1. _____
2. _____
3. _____
4. _____
5. _____
6. _____
7. _____
8. _____
9. _____
10. _____
11. _____
12. _____
13. _____
14. _____
15. _____
16. _____
17. _____
18. _____
19. _____
20. _____

1. She finished the book **report**.
2. The soldiers obeyed his **order**.
3. I need a **sword** for my costume.
4. They do **forty** laps in the pool.
5. This is an **enormous** sandwich.
6. Let's **explore** the forest.
7. It was hard to **ignore** the sound.
8. I get hungry; **therefore** I eat.
9. She is an **expert** skier.
10. The **service** station was closed.
11. Skill will **determine** the winner.
12. This is a **permanent** marker.
13. This project requires **research**.
14. I am **earning** enough money.
15. That book is **worth** reading.
16. The **worst** part is over.
17. Your research is very **thorough**.
18. Shania's mother is an **attorney**.
19. Do not **disturb** the residents.
20. Are you ready to **purchase** it?

Pretest

Notes for Home: Your child took a pretest on words that have vowel sounds with the letter *r*.
Home Activity: Help your child learn misspelled words before the final test. Have your child divide misspelled words into parts (such as syllables) and concentrate on each part.

Spelling: Vowel Sounds with *r* 13

Name _____

Hot Dogs and Bamboo Shoots

Spelling: Vowel Sounds with *r*

Word List

report	enormous	expert	research	thorough
order	explore	service	earning	attorney
sword	ignore	determine	worth	disturb
forty	therefore	permanent	worst	purchase

Directions: Choose the words from the box that have the same vowel sound as **fort**. Write each word in the correct column.

Spelled or

1. _____
2. _____
3. _____
4. _____
5. _____

Spelled ore

6. _____
7. _____
8. _____

Directions: Choose the words from the box that have the same vowel sound as **work**. Write each word in the correct column.

Spelled or

9. _____
10. _____
11. _____
12. _____

Spelled ur

13. _____
14. _____

Directions: Choose the word from the box that best completes each sentence. Write the word on the line to the left.

_____ 15. My friend Yanni is an _____ who knows everything about gardens.

_____ 16. His first book took years of study and _____.

_____ 17. Some garden designs are _____; others change every year.

_____ 18. Books provide an important _____ for home gardeners.

_____ 19. Yanni has the chance of _____ a great prize if his book is selected by the judges.

_____ 20. To _____ who will win, judges have to read all the books.

Notes for Home: Your child spelled words with the vowel sound heard in *report* and *explore*, and the vowel sound heard in *expert*, *research*, and *disturb*. **Home Activity:** Challenge your child to find other words with these two vowel sounds. Discuss how these words are spelled.

14 Spelling: Vowel Sounds with *r*

Name _____

Hot Dogs and Bamboo Shoots

Spelling: Vowel Sounds with *r*

Directions: Proofread these two Japanese *haiku* (short poems about simple images). Find five spelling mistakes. Use the proofreading marks to correct each mistake.

≡	Make a capital.
/	Make a small letter.
∧	Add something.
℘	Take out something.
⊙	Add a period.
¶	Begin a new paragraph.

Cherry Blossoms

Explore their pink blooms

See their premanent order

Wurth of fourty trees

Spelling Tip

report   worth

Watch for letter pairs that represent different vowel sounds. The letters **or** can represent two different vowel sounds, as heard in **report** and **worth.**

Battle

Enormus power

The dragonfly kills the bee

With a golden sord

Word List

report	determine
order	permanent
sword	research
forty	earning
enormous	worth
explore	worst
ignore	thorough
therefore	attorney
expert	disturb
service	purchase

Write a Haiku

On a separate sheet of paper, write a haiku of your own. A haiku always has three lines. The first and third lines have five syllables each. The second line has seven syllables. A haiku usually focuses on a single, simple image. Try to use at least three of your spelling words.

Notes for Home: Your child spelled words with the vowel sound heard in *report* and *explore,* and the vowel sound heard in *expert, research,* and *disturb.* **Home Activity:** Encourage your child to describe the haiku he or she has written. Discuss the image in the haiku.

Spelling: Vowel Sounds with *r* 15

Name _____

Hot Dogs and Bamboo Shoots

Spelling: Vowel Sounds with *r*

REVIEW

Word List

report	enormous	expert	research	thorough
order	explore	service	earning	attorney
sword	ignore	determine	worth	disturb
forty	therefore	permanent	worst	purchase

Directions: Write the word from the box that belongs in each group.

1. article, story, _____
2. blade, knife, _____
3. value, importance, _____
4. overlook, disregard, _____
5. consequently, thus, _____
6. help, aid, _____
7. twenty, thirty, _____
8. decide, conclude, _____

Directions: Choose the word from the box that is the most opposite in meaning for each word below. Write the word on the line.

9. sell _____
10. best _____
11. spending _____
12. beginner _____
13. temporary _____
14. tiny _____

Directions: Choose the word from the box that best replaces the underlined word. Write the word on the line.

_____ 15. Arrange the coins by value.

_____ 16. The biologist's study may help find a cure for a disease.

_____ 17. I am taking my cat in for a complete health check.

_____ 18. Ben is sleeping, please do not bother him.

_____ 19. Connie has an appointment with her lawyer.

_____ 20. I want to investigate where the mouse could have gone.

Notes for Home: Your child spelled words with the vowel sound heard in *report* and *explore*, and the vowel sound heard in *expert*, *research*, and *disturb*. **Home Activity:** Have your child choose a spelling word and find another word with the same vowel sound spelled the same way.

Name_____   **The Telephone Call**

Spelling: Getting Letters in Correct Order

Pretest Directions: Fold back the page along the dotted line. On the blanks, write the spelling words as they are dictated. When you have finished the test, unfold the page and check your words.

1. _____
2. _____
3. _____
4. _____
5. _____
6. _____
7. _____
8. _____
9. _____
10. _____
11. _____
12. _____
13. _____
14. _____
15. _____
16. _____
17. _____
18. _____
19. _____
20. _____

1. Her **poetry** is wonderful.
2. I smelled a **beautiful** flower.
3. His sister is **thirteen** years old.
4. The cat has a scratchy **tongue**.
5. Some **pieces** of candy were left.
6. I've saved two **thousand** dollars.
7. We walked **through** the park.
8. What an **unusual** story!
9. The **building** was torn down.
10. Mrs. Patel got a fishing **license**.
11. They will **remodel** the house.
12. She was **grateful** for the help.
13. I'm your friend, not your **enemy**.
14. What **instrument** do you play?
15. A jazz band will **perform**.
16. Do you **prefer** milk or juice?
17. My mother **judged** the dog show.
18. He **adjusted** the recliner.
19. The **soldier** laid down his gun.
20. My **neighborhood** is nearby.

Pretest

Notes for Home: Your child took a pretest on words with difficult letter combinations. *Home Activity:* Help your child learn misspelled words before the final test. See if there are any similar errors and discuss a memory trick that could help.

Spelling: Getting Letters in Correct Order 17

Name _____ The Telephone Call

Spelling: Getting Letters in Correct Order

Word List			
poetry	neighborhood	license	perform
beautiful	thousand	remodel	prefer
thirteen	through	grateful	judged
tongue	unusual	enemy	adjusted
pieces	building	instrument	soldier

Directions: Choose the word from the box that is the base word of each word below. Write the word on the line.

1. preferably _____
2. gratefulness _____
3. licensed _____
4. performance _____
5. instrumental _____
6. beautifully _____
7. remodeling _____
8. thirteenth _____

Directions: Choose the word from the box that completes each equation. Write the word on the line.

9. thought − ght + sand = _____
10. un + use − e + ual = _____
11. poem − m + try = _____
12. ad + justify − ify + ed = _____
13. pie + crust − rust + es = _____
14. judgment − ment + ed = _____
15. neigh + boring − ing + hood = _____
16. sole − e + diet − t + r = _____
17. tongs − s + ue = _____
18. the − e + rough = _____
19. energy − rgy + my = _____
20. built − t + ding = _____

Notes for Home: Your child spelled words with letter combinations that are hard to keep in order. *Home Activity:* Have your child spell each spelling word aloud. If your child mixes up some letters, give a spelling hint that will help him or her remember the correct spelling.

18 Spelling: Getting Letters in Correct Order

Name _____   **The Telephone Call**

Spelling: Getting Letters in Correct Order

Directions: Proofread this letter about a family crisis. Find seven spelling mistakes. Use the proofreading marks to correct each mistake.

≡	Make a capital.
/	Make a small letter.
∧	Add something.
⌐	Take out something.
⊙	Add a period.
¶	Begin a new paragraph.

Dear Jane,

You won't believe what happened. My father decided to remodal the bedroom himself. "You don't need a lisence to put in a couple of windows," he said.

I perfer not to think about it. I can still hear the unuzual sound he made as he fell. The sound echoed right thorugh our building. We are greatful to the people in the nieghborhood who came running. The window had broken into a thousand pieces. Luckily, the only thing seriously hurt was Dad's pride.

Write soon,

Rafael

Spelling Tip

through   prefer

Your spelling words contain letters that are hard to keep in order. Study the Word List carefully before proofreading the letter.

Word List
poetry
beautiful
thirteen
tongue
pieces
neighborhood
thousand
through
unusual
building
license
remodel
grateful
enemy
instrument
perform
prefer
judged
adjusted
soldier

Proofread and Write

Write a Letter

Imagine you are Jane. On a separate sheet of paper, write a letter to Rafael describing a family crisis and how it was solved. Try to use at least five of your spelling words.

Notes for Home: Your child spelled words with letter combinations that are hard to keep in order. **Home Activity:** Help your child to make up sentences that contain the words *perform* and *pieces*. Have your child check his or her sentences to see that all words are correctly spelled.

Name _____   The Telephone Call

Spelling: Getting Letters in Correct Order

REVIEW

Word List

poetry	pieces	unusual	grateful	prefer
beautiful	neighborhood	building	enemy	judged
thirteen	thousand	license	instrument	adjusted
tongue	through	remodel	perform	soldier

Directions: Choose the word from the box that best matches each clue. Write the word on the line.

_____ 1. I am what the parts of a jigsaw puzzle are called.

_____ 2. I am ten hundreds.

_____ 3. I am a person who serves in the army.

_____ 4. I am always between twelve and fourteen.

_____ 5. I am needed for speech.

_____ 6. I am something or someone who tries to harm.

_____ 7. I am a permit that allows a person to drive.

_____ 8. I am a group of words that sometimes rhyme.

_____ 9. I am both a place to live and a game played with blocks.

_____ 10. I am something with which you can make music.

Directions: Choose the word from the box that best matches each definition. Write the word on the line.

_____ 11. community or area

_____ 12. strange

_____ 13. decided or concluded from evidence

_____ 14. like better

_____ 15. thankful

_____ 16. lovely

_____ 17. make over

_____ 18. act or carry out

_____ 19. in one side and out the other

_____ 20. changed or fixed slightly

Notes for Home: Your child spelled words with combinations of letters that are hard to keep in order. **Home Activity:** Encourage your child to find as many shorter words within the words in the list as possible. For example, *instrument* contains *in* and *strum*.

Name _____

A Trouble-Making Crow

Spelling: Words from Many Cultures

Pretest Directions: Fold back the page along the dotted line. On the blanks, write the spelling words as they are dictated. When you have finished the test, unfold the page and check your words.

1. _____
2. _____
3. _____
4. _____
5. _____
6. _____
7. _____
8. _____
9. _____
10. _____
11. _____
12. _____
13. _____
14. _____
15. _____
16. _____
17. _____
18. _____
19. _____
20. _____

1. The **moose** has huge antlers.
2. We saw a **cobra** at the zoo.
3. The **alligator** lives in a swamp.
4. I want **vanilla** ice cream.
5. He has never eaten a **banana**.
6. **Tomato** sauce can stain clothing.
7. Please use a lot of **mustard**.
8. Her parents learned the **hula**.
9. What's in your **picnic** basket?
10. Let's have a **barbecue**.
11. It isn't wise to pet a **crocodile**.
12. The **coyote** barked at the birds.
13. A **koala** lives in this big tree.
14. She likes **macaroni** and cheese.
15. Please pass me the **catsup**.
16. They danced the **polka** all night.
17. We are going to the **ballet**.
18. My parents like to **waltz**.
19. We ate at a **banquet** hall.
20. I made two trips to the **buffet**.

Pretest

Notes for Home: Your child took a pretest on words that come from other languages. *Home Activity:* Help your child learn misspelled words before the final test. Your child should look at the word, say it, spell it aloud, and then spell it with eyes shut.

Spelling: Words from Many Cultures 21

Name _____

A Trouble-Making Crow

Spelling: Words from Many Cultures

Word List

moose	banana	picnic	koala	ballet
cobra	tomato	barbecue	macaroni	waltz
alligator	mustard	crocodile	catsup	banquet
vanilla	hula	coyote	polka	buffet

Directions: Write the words from the box that belong in each group.

Animals   **Things to Eat**   **Dances**

1. _____   7. _____   13. _____

2. _____   8. _____   14. _____

3. _____   9. _____   15. _____

4. _____   10. _____   16. _____

5. _____   11. _____

6. _____   12. _____

Directions: Choose the word from the box that best matches each clue. Write the word on the line.

_____ 17. It is both an open grill and meat cooked in a spicy sauce.

_____ 18. It is a meal eaten outdoors. Hint: Ants love them.

_____ 19. It is a meal at which people serve themselves from a sideboard or counter.

_____ 20. It is a feast or large meal with many courses.

Notes for Home: Your child spelled words that come from other languages. *Home Activity:* Challenge your child to use the spelling words to write several sentences. Have him or her check the sentences to be sure all the words are spelled correctly.

22 Spelling: Words from Many Cultures

A Trouble-Making Crow

Spelling: Words from Many Cultures

Directions: Proofread these minutes from a meeting. Find seven spelling mistakes. Use the proofreading marks to correct each mistake.

≡	Make a capital.
/	Make a small letter.
∧	Add something.
╯	Take out something.
⊙	Add a period.
¶	Begin a new paragraph.

 Minutes from August Meeting

- This summer's picnick was great. We'll plan to have another one next June.

- We ran short of catsup, musterd, relish, macaronie salad, and meat. We'll need more food, more barbaque grills, and extra cooks.

- The vanila ice cream melted. Let's try strawberry shortcake next time.

- Next year we should set up the food on a buffett table.

- The guests really enjoyed dancing, especially the waltz and poka. Let's include those dances and add others.

Word List
moose
cobra
alligator
vanilla
banana
tomato
mustard
hula
picnic
barbecue
crocodile
coyote
koala
macaroni
catsup
polka
ballet
waltz
banquet
buffet

Proofread and Write

Spelling Tip

ballet   **buffet**

Many English words come from other languages and may have unexpected spellings. **Ballet** and **buffet** are French words, so they follow the French rule that **-et** sounds like the English long **a**.

Write Minutes from a Meeting

Imagine that you are the head caretaker of a wild animal park. You hold a meeting to discuss ways to keep the animals healthy and happy. On a separate piece of paper, make a list of plans for the park. Use at least five spelling words.

 **Notes for Home:** Your child spelled words that come from other languages. *Home Activity:* Work with your child to create a crossword puzzle using several of the spelling words.

Spelling: Words from Many Cultures

Name _____

A Trouble-Making Crow

Spelling: Words from Many Cultures   REVIEW

Word List

moose	banana	picnic	koala	ballet
cobra	tomato	barbecue	macaroni	waltz
alligator	mustard	crocodile	catsup	banquet
vanilla	hula	coyote	polka	buffet

Directions: Choose the word from the box that best matches each definition. Write the word on the line.

_____ 1. a lizard-like reptile with a narrow head (Greek)

_____ 2. a large reptile with a short, flat head (Spanish)

_____ 3. a theatrical dance (French, from Italian)

_____ 4. a red or yellow juicy fruit (Nahuatl [Aztec])

_____ 5. a tube-shaped type of pasta (Italian)

_____ 6. a meal at which people serve themselves (French)

_____ 7. a large mammal with broad antlers (Algonquin)

_____ 8. a smooth, gliding dance in triple time (German)

_____ 9. a curved yellow or red tropical fruit (Spanish)

_____ 10. a yellow seasoning (French)

_____ 11. a spicy sauce made from tomatoes (Malay)

_____ 12. a lively folk dance (Polish)

Directions: Choose the word from the box that best completes each command. Write the word on the line to the left.

_____ 13. Roast the meat on the outdoor _____.

_____ 14. Hear the howling of the wild _____.

_____ 15. Plan to eat several courses at the ceremonial _____.

_____ 16. Stir the cake batter and then add the _____.

_____ 17. Please avoid stepping on that poisonous _____!

_____ 18. Look at the furry Australian _____ in the tree.

_____ 19. Put the _____ basket on that blanket under the tree.

_____ 20. Dance the graceful Hawaiian _____.

Notes for Home: Your child spelled words that come from other languages. **Home Activity:** With your child, write tongue twisters for the spelling words, such as *Minnie the Moose munched many mangoes.*

24 Spelling: Words from Many Cultures

Name _____   From a Spark

Spelling: Unexpected Consonant Spellings

Pretest Directions: Fold back the page along the dotted line. On the blanks, write the spelling words as they are dictated. When you have finished the test, unfold the page and check your words.

1. _____
2. _____
3. _____
4. _____
5. _____
6. _____
7. _____
8. _____
9. _____
10. _____
11. _____
12. _____
13. _____
14. _____
15. _____
16. _____
17. _____
18. _____
19. _____
20. _____

1. I don't **doubt** your excuse.
2. Strange movies **fascinate** her.
3. He enjoys his **science** classes.
4. We drove along a **scenic** route.
5. Leaves change colors in **autumn**.
6. He writes a daily **column**.
7. The defendant is not **guilty**.
8. Our soccer **league** is a big one.
9. Her brother was her **guardian**.
10. The spy wore a clever **disguise**.
11. His jokes are very **subtle**.
12. They were in **debt** to the bank.
13. I enjoy **reminiscent** music.
14. The cliff makes a steep **descent**.
15. I **condemn** cruelty to animals.
16. This is a **solemn** occasion.
17. Sometimes you need **guidance**.
18. Your meaning is **vague**.
19. The hikers battled **fatigue**.
20. I like books filled with **intrigue**.

Pretest

Notes for Home: Your child took a pretest on words with unexpected combinations of consonants. *Home Activity:* Help your child learn misspelled words before the final test. Your child can underline the word parts that caused the problems and concentrate on those parts.

Spelling: Unexpected Consonant Spellings   25

Name _____ From a Spark

Spelling: Unexpected Consonant Spellings

Word List				
doubt	autumn	guardian	reminiscent	guidance
fascinate	column	disguise	descent	vague
science	guilty	subtle	condemn	fatigue
scenic	league	debt	solemn	intrigue

Directions: Choose the words from the box spelled with **bt, gue,** and **gu.** Listen for the consonant sound each group of letters represents. Write each word in the correct column.

Words spelled bt

1. _____
2. _____
3. _____

Words spelled gue

4. _____
5. _____
6. _____
7. _____

Words spelled gu

8. _____
9. _____
10. _____
11. _____

Directions: Choose the word from the box that best completes each sentence. Write the word on the line to the left.

_____ 12. The desert sunrise provided a _____ view as we entered the mine.

_____ 13. We went exploring this _____ to avoid the colder temperatures of winter.

_____ 14. Gradually, we began the _____ down the steep slope.

_____ 15. Fred looked serious and _____ as daylight faded behind us.

_____ 16. We had read the studies in the _____ journals about the atmosphere inside old mine shafts.

_____ 17. Our group had to decide whether to _____ the property as unsuitable for future use.

_____ 18. The mine was _____ of a scene from an old movie.

_____ 19. Each sturdy _____ helped hold up the rough ceiling.

_____ 20. The complexity of the mine would amaze and _____ anyone.

Notes for Home: Your child spelled words with unexpected letter combinations. *Home Activity:* Help your child sort the spelling words into groups that contain the letters *sc, bt, gu* or *gue,* and *mn.* Each letter group represents one consonant sound.

26 Spelling: Unexpected Consonant Spellings

Name _____   From a Spark

Spelling: Unexpected Consonant Spellings

Directions: Proofread this journal entry. Find six spelling mistakes. Use the proofreading marks to correct each mistake.

> **Day 3.** It's great to be back up top again. We just finished the hardest desent into the caves to date, and all my muscles ache with fatige. But today we found a cavern sure to fascinat even the most experienced explorer! After hours of climbing and crawling through mud in temperatures reminiscint of a refrigerator, I began to dout my abilities. Finally, I squeezed my way through a narrow passage into a huge chamber. Our lights shone on an enormous limestone colum. Now I understand the intrigue of cave exploration!

≡ Make a capital.
/ Make a small letter.
∧ Add something.
⌢ Take out something.
⊙ Add a period.
¶ Begin a new paragraph.

Word List
doubt
fascinate
science
scenic
autumn
column
guilty
league
guardian
disguise
subtle
debt
reminiscent
descent
condemn
solemn
guidance
vague
fatigue
intrigue

Spelling Tip

fascinate   fatigue
Fa<u>sc</u>inate, fati<u>gue</u>, and other spelling words use two or more letters to stand for one consonant sound. Make sure they are spelled correctly in the journal entry.

Write a Journal Entry

On a separate sheet of paper, write a journal entry describing a wilderness adventure. Imagine that you are exploring a new territory. Have you had any narrow escapes? How did you survive? How did you feel when you finally reached your goal? Try to use at least five of your spelling words.

Notes for Home: Your child spelled words with unexpected letter combinations. **Home Activity:** Have your child read the spelling words for you to write. Then have your child check your spelling.

Proofread and Write

Spelling: Unexpected Consonant Spellings   **27**

Name _____   From a Spark

Spelling: Unexpected Consonant Spellings

REVIEW

Word List				
doubt	autumn	guardian	reminiscent	guidance
fascinate	column	disguise	descent	vague
science	guilty	subtle	condemn	fatigue
scenic	league	debt	solemn	intrigue

Directions: Write the word from the box that belongs in each group.

1. pillar, post, _____
2. unclear, not distinct, _____
3. beautiful, natural, _____
4. costume, mask, _____
5. grave, serious, _____
6. direction, leadership, _____
7. caretaker, protector, _____
8. plot, scheme, _____
9. judge, convict, _____
10. remembered, suggestive, _____
11. interest, charm, _____

Directions: Choose the word from the box that best matches each clue. Write the word on the line.

_____ 12. It's not obvious so you might just overlook me.

_____ 13. It's the season between summer and winter.

_____ 14. It includes the subjects chemistry, biology, and physics.

_____ 15. It's a group of people or a division in sports.

_____ 16. It's what you feel when you don't know for sure.

_____ 17. It's the opposite of *innocent*.

_____ 18. It's how you would describe a beautiful view.

_____ 19. It's money or other items owed to someone.

_____ 20. It's a trip downstairs, down a hill, or down a mountain.

Notes for Home: Your child spelled words with unexpected letter combinations. *Home Activity:* Give your child clues about each spelling word. Have your child identify and spell each word. For example: *You use a costume to do this.* (disguise)

28 Spelling: Unexpected Consonant Spellings

Name _____ Storm-a-Dust

Spelling: Compound Words 1

Pretest Directions: Fold back the page along the dotted line. On the blanks, write the spelling words as they are dictated. When you have finished the test, unfold the page and check your words.

1. _____	1. I went to the library by **myself**.
2. _____	2. They always enjoy **themselves**.
3. _____	3. The **hallway** was long.
4. _____	4. Who is your **homeroom** teacher?
5. _____	5. They want to know **everything**.
6. _____	6. I have a **teenage** brother.
7. _____	7. One **teammate** was late.
8. _____	8. She has a new **skateboard**.
9. _____	9. **Everybody** came to the party.
10. _____	10. Your dog ate my **doughnut**.
11. _____	11. **Ice cream** is best on hot days.
12. _____	12. I changed in the **locker room**.
13. _____	13. I bought a new **tape recorder**.
14. _____	14. Let's have **root beer** floats.
15. _____	15. This street is a **dead end**.
16. _____	16. Can you fix the **air conditioner**?
17. _____	17. His father has a **polka dot** tie.
18. _____	18. I love the new **roller coaster**.
19. _____	19. Put an **ice pack** on your bruise.
20. _____	20. What is the **solar system**?

Pretest

Notes for Home: Your child took a pretest on compound words written as one word and as two words. *Home Activity:* Help your child learn misspelled words before the final test. Dictate the word and have your child spell the word aloud for you or write it on paper.

Spelling: Compound Words 1   29

Name_____   Storm-a-Dust

Spelling: Compound Words 1

Word List

myself	teenage	ice cream	air conditioner
themselves	teammate	locker room	polka dot
hallway	skateboard	tape recorder	roller coaster
homeroom	everybody	root beer	ice pack
everything	doughnut	dead end	solar system

Directions: Add a word to each word below to form a compound word from the box. Write the compound word on the line.

1. root _____
2. my _____
3. air _____
4. dead _____
5. roller _____

6. body _____
7. polka _____
8. them _____
9. cream _____
10. team _____

Directions: Find the two words in each sentence that make up a compound word from the box. Write the compound word on the line.

_____ 11. My locker is near the weight room.

_____ 12. Boxes blocked the hall, but he found a way past.

_____ 13. Fill the cooler with ice before you pack the food and drinks.

_____ 14. We listened to a tape of a recorder, flute, and guitar.

_____ 15. He had to go home and clean his room.

_____ 16. The solar panel was near the heating system.

_____ 17. She loved to skate fast down the big wooden board.

_____ 18. After shaping the dough into small pieces, place a nut on each piece.

_____ 19. She asked the teen to state his age.

_____ 20. Mom thought every child deserved at least one cute thing for a door prize.

Notes for Home: Your child spelled compound words written as one word and as two words.
Home Activity: Take turns saying one part of one of the compound words from the Word List. The other person names the compound word and spells it.

Name_____

Storm-a-Dust

Spelling: Compound Words 1

Directions: Proofread this story. Find six spelling mistakes. Use the proofreading marks to correct each mistake.

Danny and his family had crouched in their halway closet as the tornado passed by. After the storm, Danny went outside and joined all the neighbors who lived on their ded end street. They were talking among themselves about the damage. It seemed as if evrything had been tossed around. Wet papers made polkadot patterns everywhere. An air conditioner had been blown through a window at the home of Danny's teamate Willie. Luckily, no one had been hurt. And amazingly, a skate board still sat in the yard where someone had left it before the storm.

≡ Make a capital.
/ Make a small letter.
∧ Add something.
⌒ Take out something.
⊙ Add a period.
¶ Begin a new paragraph.

Spelling Tip
Some compounds are closed and are written as one word: **everything.** Others are open and are written as two words: **air conditioner.**

Word List
myself
themselves
hallway
homeroom
everything
teenage
teammate
skateboard
everybody
doughnut
ice cream
locker room
tape recorder
root beer
dead end
air conditioner
polka dot
roller coaster
ice pack
solar system

Write a Short Story
On a separate sheet of paper, write a short story that describes the effects of a flood, a blizzard, or other violent storm. Include the characters' reactions and explain how it changed their lives. Try to use at least five spelling words.

Notes for Home: Your child spelled compound words written as one word and as two words, such as *everybody* and *tape recorder*. **Home Activity:** Encourage your child to find the compound words in a short newspaper article. Make a list of these compound words.

Name_____   Storm-a-Dust

Spelling: Compound Words 1   REVIEW

Word List

myself	teenage	ice cream	air conditioner
themselves	teammate	locker room	polka dot
hallway	skateboard	tape recorder	roller coaster
homeroom	everybody	root beer	ice pack
everything	doughnut	dead end	solar system

Directions: Write the word from the box that belongs in each group.

1. pastry, turnover, _____
2. bike, roller skates, _____
3. galaxy, universe, _____
4. gym, stadium, _____
5. Ferris wheel, carousel, _____
6. lobby, corridor, _____
7. freezer, refrigerator, _____
8. stripe, plaid, _____
9. turntable, CD player, _____
10. choir room, assembly room, _____

Directions: Choose the word from the box that best completes each song title. Write the word on the line to the left. Be sure to capitalize each important word.

_____ 11. "A Bandage for My Heart and an _____ for My Soul"

_____ 12. "Two Straws Sticking in a _____ Float"

_____ 13. "Why Does _____ Clown Around in Class?"

_____ 14. "Just Too Young to Be a _____ Superstar"

_____ 15. "Scoop Me Up Another _____ Cone!"

_____ 16. "I'm Lonesome and Lonely All by _____"

_____ 17. "Just One More _____ Street"

_____ 18. "They'll Have to Move It by _____"

_____ 19. "_____ Is Better Now That You're Here"

_____ 20. "My _____ and I Can Win Any Game"

Notes for Home: Your child spelled compound words written as one word and as two words, such as *everybody* and *tape recorder*. **Home Activity:** Write each part of a compound word on a slip of paper. Draw two slips and try to form a compound word.

32 Spelling: Compound Words 1

Name _____

The Day of the Turtle

Spelling: Compound Words 2

Pretest Directions: Fold back the page along the dotted line. On the blanks, write the spelling words as they are dictated. When you have finished the test, unfold the page and check your words.

1. _____	1. The **basketball** game was close.
2. _____	2. We looked **everywhere** for him.
3. _____	3. The cat went **outside**.
4. _____	4. **Summertime** is always nice.
5. _____	5. I forgot **something** at home.
6. _____	6. She said it as an **afterthought**.
7. _____	7. My sister is a **cheerleader**.
8. _____	8. The **quarterback** was tackled.
9. _____	9. This old **bookstore** is wonderful.
10. _____	10. He works at the **courthouse**.
11. _____	11. She had to **baby-sit** her brother.
12. _____	12. Let's go **roller-skating** tomorrow.
13. _____	13. The old **drive-in** theater closed.
14. _____	14. You must learn **self-control**.
15. _____	15. He has a **part-time** job.
16. _____	16. We **ice-skated** for an hour.
17. _____	17. My aunt is **ninety-five** years old.
18. _____	18. Her **brother-in-law** is a pilot.
19. _____	19. We **water-skied** all day.
20. _____	20. I like **old-fashioned** clothing.

Pretest

Notes for Home: Your child took a pretest on compound words with and without hyphens.
Home Activity: Help your child learn misspelled words. He or she can divide misspelled words into parts (such as syllables), concentrate on each part, and notice if there is a hyphen.

Spelling: Compound Words 2 33

Name _____

The Day of the Turtle

Spelling: Compound Words 2

Think and Practice

Word List				
basketball	something	bookstore	drive-in	ninety-five
everywhere	afterthought	courthouse	self-control	brother-in-law
outside	cheerleader	baby-sit	part-time	water-skied
summertime	quarterback	roller-skating	ice-skated	old-fashioned

Directions: Choose a word from the box that best answers each question. Write the word on the line.

_____ 1. What is the opposite of *modern*?

_____ 2. What would be an excellent test score?

_____ 3. When do schoolchildren have lots of free time?

_____ 4. What helps a person keep his or her temper?

_____ 5. What do you have if you have more than nothing?

_____ 6. How do you describe a job you only go to on weekends?

_____ 7. Which word names an idea that comes too late?

Directions: Write the words from the box that belong in each group.

Places

8. _____
9. _____
10. _____
11. _____
12. _____

People

13. _____
14. _____
15. _____

Activities

16. _____
17. _____
18. _____
19. _____
20. _____

Notes for Home: Your child spelled compound words with and without hyphens and compounds made up of a noun and a verb. **Home Activity:** Read a newspaper with your child. Make a list of compound words you find.

34 Spelling: Compound Words 2

Spelling: Compound Words 2

Directions: Proofread this news story. Find six spelling mistakes. Use the proofreading marks to correct each mistake.

Proofreading marks
≡ Make a capital.
/ Make a small letter.
∧ Add something.
⌒ Take out something.
⊙ Add a period.
¶ Begin a new paragraph.

Local Students Save Dog

A small dog named Wylie had a quarter-back and a cheer-leader to thank for saving his life. According to Stan Nagy, the dog's owner and brother-in law to the mayor, Wylie chased something into a pipe on a street. As temperatures out side soared above ninety-five degrees, the little dog couldn't get out. Luckily, Paul Woud and Yassi Levine were roller-skating to a nearby drivin restaurant when they heard Wylie bark. Levine, a partime clerk's intern at the courthouse, alerted the police, who freed Wylie.

Word List
- basketball
- everywhere
- outside
- summertime
- something
- afterthought
- cheerleader
- quarterback
- bookstore
- courthouse
- baby-sit
- roller-skating
- drive-in
- self-control
- part-time
- ice-skated
- ninety-five
- brother-in-law
- water-skied
- old-fashioned

Spelling Tip
Remember to keep all the letters when writing a closed compound word. Use hyphens for numbers twenty-one to ninety-nine, compounds ending with **in-law,** compounds beginning with **self,** and compounds made up of a noun and a verb.

Write a News Story
On a separate sheet of paper, write a news story about an animal rescue. Try to use at least five of your spelling words.

Notes for Home: Your child spelled compound words with and without hyphens and compounds made up of a noun and a verb. *Home Activity:* Take turns naming other compounds that contain one of the shorter words that make up the compounds in the Word List.

Name _____

The Day of the Turtle

Spelling: Compound Words 2

REVIEW

Word List

basketball	something	bookstore	drive-in	ninety-five
everywhere	afterthought	courthouse	self-control	brother-in-law
outside	cheerleader	baby-sit	part-time	water-skied
summertime	quarterback	roller-skating	ice-skated	old-fashioned

Directions: Choose the word from the box that includes the underlined part of each word below. Write the word on the line.

1. twenty-<u>five</u> _____
2. <u>law</u>-abiding _____
3. <u>after</u>noon _____
4. <u>self</u>-pity _____
5. no<u>where</u> _____

6. waste<u>basket</u> _____
7. every<u>thing</u> _____
8. <u>drive</u>-through _____
9. shut<u>out</u> _____
10. story<u>book</u> _____

Directions: Choose a word from the box that best completes each person's statement. Write the word on the line to the left.

_____ 11. Big brother: "Sure, Mom. I'll _____ the kids tonight."
_____ 12. Football player: "If the _____ passes me the ball, I'll run."
_____ 13. Judge: "My office can be found in the county _____."
_____ 14. Little girl: "I want to go to the _____ party at the rink."
_____ 15. Coach: "To be a _____, you must have pep and team spirit."
_____ 16. Boater: "We _____ up and down the lake all afternoon."
_____ 17. Antique dealer: "People really love _____ gadgets."
_____ 18. Student: "To earn a little money, I work _____ in the fall."
_____ 19. Lifeguard: "The outdoor pool is open daily in the _____."
_____ 20. Hockey player: "I've _____ since the day I learned to walk."

Notes for Home: Your child spelled compound words with and without hyphens and compounds made up of a noun and a verb. **Home Activity:** Challenge your child to write the hyphenated compounds from the list in alphabetical order.

Name_____

Saving the Sound

Spelling: Words with No Sound Clues

Pretest Directions: Fold back the page along the dotted line. On the blanks, write the spelling words as they are dictated. When you have finished the test, unfold the page and check your words.

1. _____
2. _____
3. _____
4. _____
5. _____
6. _____
7. _____
8. _____
9. _____
10. _____
11. _____
12. _____
13. _____
14. _____
15. _____
16. _____
17. _____
18. _____
19. _____
20. _____

1. I'm **interested** in beekeeping.
2. They **usually** arrive early.
3. She drove an **American** car.
4. We walked **toward** the ocean.
5. The café is a family **business**.
6. I had **vegetable** soup for lunch.
7. This book is **really** mine.
8. His house stood **opposite** theirs.
9. The hike up the hill was **difficult**.
10. Will it be **Christmas** soon?
11. She bought a sports **magazine**.
12. Please **apologize** to him.
13. Try to **multiply** the figures.
14. **Jealousy** is a strong emotion.
15. The conclusion was **elementary**.
16. We cannot live without **oxygen**.
17. He grew up in **Maryland**.
18. This is a **sensitive** matter.
19. **Laughter** can be contagious.
20. Cancer is a terrible **disease**.

Pretest

Notes for Home: Your child took a pretest on words that give no sound clues as to their spelling. *Home Activity:* Help your child learn misspelled words before the final test. Your child should look at the word, say it, spell it aloud, and then spell it with eyes shut.

Spelling: Words with No Sound Clues   37

Spelling: Words with No Sound Clues

Word List

interested	vegetable	magazine	oxygen
usually	really	apologize	Maryland
American	opposite	multiply	sensitive
toward	difficult	jealousy	laughter
business	Christmas	elementary	disease

Directions: Choose the word from the box that contains each word below. Write the word on the line. Use each word only once.

1. site _____
2. sit _____
3. usual _____
4. real _____
5. bus _____
6. ease _____
7. can _____
8. log _____
9. tip _____
10. tar _____

Directions: Choose the word from the box that best matches each definition. Write the word on the line.

_____ 11. a publication with stories and articles
_____ 12. envy
_____ 13. happy sound
_____ 14. attentive; not bored
_____ 15. in the direction of
_____ 16. an east-coast state
_____ 17. December 25
_____ 18. an edible plant
_____ 19. hard
_____ 20. a gas in the air

Notes for Home: Your child spelled words with letters that give no sound clues as to their spelling, such as *vegetable, business,* and *opposite.* **Home Activity:** Challenge your child to sort words from the list into groups according to the number of syllables the words contain.

38 Spelling: Words with No Sound Clues

Name _____

Saving the Sound

Spelling: Words with No Sound Clues

Directions: Proofread these interview questions for a news article. Find five spelling mistakes. Use the proofreading marks to correct each mistake.

≡ Make a capital.
/ Make a small letter.
∧ Add something.
⌒ Take out something.
⊙ Add a period.
¶ Begin a new paragraph.

1. Why should the American public still be intrested in the oil spill after more than ten years?

2. Which animals do not usully recover from the spill?

3. Magezine articles have said that some plants were more likely to die from dusease than others. Please explain.

4. Is the oil spill affecting the fishing busnes in the region? If so, in what way?

Word List
interested
usually
American
toward
business
vegetable
really
opposite
difficult
Christmas
magazine
apologize
multiply
jealousy
elementary
oxygen
Maryland
sensitive
laughter
disease

Spelling Tip

business   magazine

Some words in the list have letters for sounds that you don't hear: bus<u>i</u>ness. Other words in the list have vowel sounds that give no clue to their spelling: mag<u>a</u>zine.

Write Interview Questions

Imagine that you need to interview experts who are cleaning up an oil spill. On a separate sheet of paper, write several questions you would ask to find out more about the accident and cleanup efforts. Try to use at least five of your spelling words.

Notes for Home: Your child spelled words with letters that give no sound clues as to their spelling. *Home Activity:* Hold a spelling bee with family and friends, taking turns spelling each word aloud.

Spelling: Words with No Sound Clues   39

Name _____ Saving the Sound

Spelling: Words with No Sound Clues REVIEW

Word List				
interested	business	difficult	multiply	Maryland
usually	vegetable	Christmas	jealousy	sensitive
American	really	magazine	elementary	laughter
toward	opposite	apologize	oxygen	disease

Directions: Choose the word from the box that is the most opposite in meaning for each word below. Write the word on the line.

1. health _____
2. hard-hearted _____
3. divide _____
4. rarely _____
5. insult _____
6. away _____
7. bored _____
8. easy _____
9. pleasure _____
10. same _____

Directions: Choose the word from the box that best matches each clue. Write the letters of the word on the blanks. The boxed letters tell why the bee went to see a doctor.

11. a weekly or monthly publication ___ ___ ___ ___ ☐ ___ ___ ___ ___
12. grade school ___ ___ ___ ___ ___ ___ ___ ☐ ___ ___
13. a reaction to a good joke ___ ___ ___ ___ ☐ ___ ___ ___
14. actually; truly ___ ___ ☐ ___ ___ ___
15. one of the fifty states ___ ___ ___ ___ ☐ ___ ___ ___ ___
16. a December holiday ___ ☐ ___ ___ ___ ___ ___ ___ ___
17. a United States citizen ___ ☐ ___ ___ ___ ___ ___ ___ ___
18. grown in a garden ___ ___ ___ ☐ ___ ___ ___ ___ ___ ___
19. the gas we breathe ___ ___ ☐ ___ ___ ___ ___
20. envy ___ ___ ___ ___ ☐ ___ ___ ___

Why did the bee go to see a doctor? _____

Notes for Home: Your child spelled words with letters that give no sound clues as to their spelling. **Home Activity:** Help your child create a crossword puzzle using as many spelling words as possible.

Name_____

Elizabeth Blackwell: Medical Pioneer

Spelling: Suffixes -ance, -ence, -ant, -ent

Pretest Directions: Fold back the page along the dotted line. On the blanks, write the spelling words as they are dictated. When you have finished the test, unfold the page and check your words.

1. _____
2. _____
3. _____
4. _____
5. _____
6. _____
7. _____
8. _____
9. _____
10. _____
11. _____
12. _____
13. _____
14. _____
15. _____
16. _____
17. _____
18. _____
19. _____
20. _____

1. Where is the main **entrance**?
2. Their **performance** starts soon.
3. I admire your car's **appearance**.
4. We went to the **clearance** sale.
5. Car **insurance** can be expensive.
6. We celebrate **Independence** Day.
7. What's the **difference**?
8. I envy her **excellence** in art.
9. He speaks with great **confidence**.
10. The friends met by **coincidence**.
11. What a **brilliant** idea!
12. My family is **important** to me.
13. Car exhaust is an air **pollutant**.
14. He made an **ignorant** remark.
15. At first, I was **hesitant** to go.
16. Dolphins are **intelligent** animals.
17. Her anger was very **apparent**.
18. The salesman was **persistent**.
19. What time's **convenient** for you?
20. He's a very **consistent** student.

Pretest

Notes for Home: Your child took a pretest on words ending in the suffixes *-ance, -ence, -ant,* and *-ent.* **Home Activity:** Help your child learn misspelled words before the final test. Your child should look at the word, say it, spell it aloud, and then spell it with eyes shut.

Spelling: Suffixes -ance, -ence, -ant, -ent   41

Elizabeth Blackwell: Medical Pioneer

Name _____

Spelling: Suffixes -ance, -ence, -ant, -ent

Word List

entrance	independence	brilliant	intelligent
performance	difference	important	apparent
appearance	excellence	pollutant	persistent
clearance	confidence	ignorant	convenient
insurance	coincidence	hesitant	consistent

Directions: Choose the words from the box that have the suffixes **-ance** or **-ence**. Write each word in the correct column.

Words Ending -ance

1. _____
2. _____
3. _____
4. _____
5. _____

Words Ending -ence

6. _____
7. _____
8. _____
9. _____
10. _____

Directions: Choose the word from the box that best matches each definition. Write the word on the line.

_____ 11. significant; meaningful

_____ 12. not giving up

_____ 13. always the same

_____ 14. lacking knowledge

_____ 15. doubtful; undecided

_____ 16. something that dirties

_____ 17. handy; nearby

_____ 18. sparkling; dazzling

_____ 19. obvious

_____ 20. smart

Notes for Home: Your child spelled words ending in the suffixes *-ance, -ence, -ant,* and *-ent*.
Home Activity: Have your child tell which three words are the most difficult to remember how to spell. Help her or him think up memory clues such as *You don't need an A to spell excellence.*

Elizabeth Blackwell: Medical Pioneer

Name_____

Spelling: Suffixes -ance, -ence, -ant, -ent

Directions: Proofread this profile of aviation pioneer Amelia Earhart. Find six spelling mistakes. Use the proofreading marks to correct each mistake.

- ≡ Make a capital.
- / Make a small letter.
- ∧ Add something.
- ⌒ Take out something.
- ⊙ Add a period.
- ¶ Begin a new paragraph.

Amelia Earhart is one pilot who made an important diferance for women everywhere. Her independance of spirit inspired women all over the country to have more confidance in their abilities to try new things. Despite early setbacks, Amelia Earhart was persitant in her efforts to make her dreams of flying come true. She was the first woman to fly solo across the Atlantic Ocean and she did it in record time! Because of her brillant performance as a pilot, it became apparent to many people that women could do whatever they had the courage to try.

Word List
entrance
performance
appearance
clearance
insurance
independence
difference
excellence
confidence
coincidence
brilliant
important
pollutant
ignorant
hesitant
intelligent
apparent
persistent
convenient
consistent

Spelling Tip
apparent
There are often no sound clues to let you know whether to use an **a** or an **e** when adding the suffixes **-ance, -ence, -ant,** and **-ent**. Make up clues to help you remember the correct spelling, such as: There is always a **parent** in app**arent**.

Write a Paragraph
On a separate sheet of paper, write a description of a real or imaginary female pioneer. Try to use at least five of your spelling words.

Notes for Home: Your child spelled words ending in the suffixes -ance, -ence, -ant, and -ent. **Home Activity:** Have your child name additional words that are spelled with -ence, such as sentence. Together, make a list of these words and check their spellings in a dictionary.

Spelling: Suffixes -ance, -ence, -ant, -ent

Name _____

Elizabeth Blackwell: Medical Pioneer

Spelling: Suffixes -ance, -ence, -ant, -ent

REVIEW

Word List

entrance	insurance	confidence	pollutant	apparent
performance	independence	coincidence	ignorant	persistent
appearance	difference	brilliant	hesitant	convenient
clearance	excellence	important	intelligent	consistent

Directions: Choose the word from the box that best completes each sentence. Write the words on the matching numbered lines to the right.

It was not a **1.** _____ that the opening **2.** _____ of Andrew McCoy's new play was on Friday the thirteenth. Early misfortunes, including the discovery of a toxic **3.** _____ in the theater's cooling system, undermined people's **4.** _____ that the play would ever open. **5.** _____ rumors that the play was jinxed have plagued the producers from the start. They also had to wait for the money from the **6.** _____ company to cover costs of water damage to the sets. At last, they were given **7.** _____ to go ahead with the performance. The **8.** _____ of the sets and costumes when the curtain was raised made the audience praise the **9.** _____ of the design. The next **10.** _____ job that remains is to bring in large crowds.

1. _____
2. _____
3. _____
4. _____
5. _____
6. _____
7. _____
8. _____
9. _____
10. _____

Directions: Choose a word from the box that is the most opposite in meaning for each word or words below. Write the word on the line. Use each word only once.

11. dull _____
12. dependence _____
13. similarity _____
14. always changing _____
15. out of the way _____
16. exit _____
17. knowing _____
18. certain _____
19. dumb _____
20. hidden _____

Notes for Home: Your child reviewed words ending in the suffixes *-ance, -ence, -ant,* and *-ent*. **Home Activity:** Challenge your child to use words ending in *-ance* to make up a rhyme.

44 Spelling: Suffixes *-ance, -ence, -ant, -ent*

Name _____   **Born Worker**

Spelling: Irregular Plurals

Pretest Directions: Fold back the page along the dotted line. On the blanks, write the spelling words as they are dictated. When you have finished the test, unfold the page and check your words.

1. _____
2. _____
3. _____
4. _____
5. _____
6. _____
7. _____
8. _____
9. _____
10. _____
11. _____
12. _____
13. _____
14. _____
15. _____
16. _____
17. _____
18. _____
19. _____
20. _____

1. These **scarfs** are made of wool.
2. Schools have teaching **staffs**.
3. This town has had ten **sheriffs**.
4. Sea animals make coral **reefs**.
5. He's met **chiefs** from many tribes.
6. The store's **shelves** are empty.
7. **Wolves** are fascinating animals.
8. We tend to keep to **ourselves**.
9. His father collects old **knives**.
10. The train was robbed by **thieves**.
11. She usually sings **solos**.
12. This store sells car **stereos**.
13. The art **studios** are downstairs.
14. **Volcanoes** erupt from time to time.
15. We bought a new set of **dominoes**.
16. The **buffaloes** grazed peacefully.
17. These spelling **quizzes** are easy!
18. Please sew up this rip in my **pants**.
19. Where did you put the **scissors**?
20. **Measles** are contagious.

Pretest

Notes for Home: Your child took a pretest on words that are irregular plurals. **Home Activity:** Help your child learn misspelled words before the final test. Your child can underline the word parts that caused the problems and concentrate on those parts.

Spelling: Irregular Plurals   45

Name _____   **Born Worker**

Spelling: Irregular Plurals

Word List			
scarfs	shelves	solos	buffaloes
staffs	wolves	stereos	quizzes
sheriffs	ourselves	studios	pants
reefs	knives	volcanoes	scissors
chiefs	thieves	dominoes	measles

Directions: Choose the words from the box where **-s** or **-es** was added to words ending in **o** and where **f** was changed to **v** before **-es** was added. Write each word in the correct column.

Plurals of Words ending in -o

1. _____
2. _____
3. _____
4. _____
5. _____
6. _____

Plurals ending in -ves

7. _____
8. _____
9. _____
10. _____
11. _____

Directions: Choose the word from the box that is the plural of the word in ( ) in each sentence. Write the word on the line.

_____ 12. Doctor: "I'm afraid these spots look like (measles)."

_____ 13. Tailor: "I have to shorten these (pants) to make them fit."

_____ 14. Student: "Please help me study for the two (quiz) tomorrow!"

_____ 15. Bosses: "Both our (staff) of workers deserve raises in pay."

_____ 16. Governor: "The (sheriff) of those three counties are corrupt."

_____ 17. Seamstress: "Help! All my pairs of (scissors) are missing!"

_____ 18. Sioux Leaders: "The (chief) of the tribes must decide what to do."

_____ 19. Diver: "The coral I saw in the (reef) of Australia is beautiful."

_____ 20. Model: "Which of these two (scarf) goes best with this coat?"

Notes for Home: Your child spelled the plurals of words ending in *o, f,* and *ff,* and words that have the same singular and plural form, such as *pants.* **Home Activity:** Have your child name the spelling words whose singular and plural forms are spelled alike.

46 Spelling: Irregular Plurals

Name _____

Born Worker

Spelling: Irregular Plurals

Directions: Proofread this interview with a Hollywood handyman. Find five spelling mistakes. Use the proofreading marks to correct each mistake.

≡ Make a capital.
/ Make a small letter.
∧ Add something.
⌐ Take out something.
⊙ Add a period.
¶ Begin a new paragraph.

Interviewer: What are some of the everyday jobs of a handyman?

Handyman: I often sharpen knifes and scissors, put up shelfs, and repair stereoes.

Interviewer: What are some of the more unusual jobs that you have been hired to do?

Handyman: Well, working for the movie studios, I repair reefs and volcanos . . . models, that is. Once I built a four-foot-tall wall out of dominos. I think my strangest job was painting measles on plastic model heads.

Spelling Tip
stereos   volcanoes

Some words that end in **o** are made plural by adding the **-s,** while others use **-es.** Check the interview to make sure the plural forms of words ending in **o** are spelled correctly.

Word List
scarfs	solos
staffs	stereos
sheriffs	studios
reefs	volcanoes
chiefs	dominoes
shelves	buffaloes
wolves	quizzes
ourselves	pants
knives	scissors
thieves	measles

Write an Interview

Imagine that you have to interview someone with an interesting job. On a separate sheet of paper, write the questions you will ask and make up the subject's responses. Try to use at least five of your spelling words.

Notes for Home: Your child spelled the plurals of words ending in *o, f,* and *ff,* and words that have the same singular and plural forms, such as *pants.* **Home Activity:** Give your child the singular form of each spelling word. Have your child name and spell the plural form.

Spelling: Irregular Plurals

Name _____   **Born Worker**

Spelling: Irregular Plurals

REVIEW

Word List

scarfs	chiefs	knives	studios	quizzes
staffs	shelves	thieves	volcanoes	pants
sheriffs	wolves	solos	dominoes	scissors
reefs	ourselves	stereos	buffaloes	measles

Directions: Choose the words from the box that best complete each story. Write the words on the matching numbered lines to the right.

Theft

1. _____ and TVs are missing. The silver forks, spoons, and 2. _____ are gone. The 3. _____ are on their way from the station to get a list of what was taken. The 4. _____ are on the run with the loot. Will we ever see our belongings again?

Rainy-Day Fun

We can play a game of 5. _____ or use 6. _____ to cut out pictures and paste them into the scrapbook. We can read about the wild 7. _____ on the plains, or listen to the 8. _____ Louis likes to play on his trumpet.

1. _____
2. _____
3. _____
4. _____
5. _____
6. _____
7. _____
8. _____

Directions: Choose the word from the box that best matches each clue. Write the word on the line.

_____ 9. We look like mountains, and we spout lava and flames.

_____ 10. We hold books, dishes, and other belongings.

_____ 11. We rule tribes and other groups of people.

_____ 12. We wrap around your neck and keep you warm.

_____ 13. We contain questions that you have to answer.

_____ 14. We are garments that cover your legs.

_____ 15. We are spots that itch.

_____ 16. We are groups of people who work for a boss.

_____ 17. We are just us.

_____ 18. We are the wild cousins of dogs.

_____ 19. We are rooms in which artists work and live.

_____ 20. We are underwater formations of coral.

Notes for Home: Your child spelled the plurals of words ending in *o, f,* and *ff,* and words that have the same singular and plural forms, such as *pants*. **Home Activity:** Help your child identify the spelling words whose plurals were formed by changing the letter *f* to *v* before adding *-es*.

Name_____   **Wilma Unlimited**

Spelling: Vowels in Unstressed Syllables

Pretest Directions: Fold back the page along the dotted line. On the blanks, write the spelling words as they are dictated. When you have finished the test, unfold the page and check your words.

1. _____
2. _____
3. _____
4. _____
5. _____
6. _____
7. _____
8. _____
9. _____
10. _____
11. _____
12. _____
13. _____
14. _____
15. _____
16. _____
17. _____
18. _____
19. _____
20. _____

1. A boat is **different** from a car.
2. We're going to **register** to vote.
3. A **carnival** is coming to town.
4. I like a wide **variety** of music.
5. A party has a festive **atmosphere**.
6. This is my **favorite** book.
7. I **pattern** myself after my father.
8. We **understand** each other.
9. That **sentence** makes no sense.
10. I can think of no similar **instance**.
11. We ate at an **elegant** restaurant.
12. Our fish need a bigger **aquarium**.
13. We **communicate** by e-mail.
14. **Gasoline** is highly flammable.
15. What do they make at the **factory**?
16. Can you give a **definite** answer?
17. I grew up in **Chicago**.
18. He slumped **heavily** into his seat.
19. We had a **garage** sale last year.
20. Who will **illustrate** your book?

Pretest

Notes for Home: Your child took a pretest on words that have indistinct vowel sounds in unstressed syllables. **Home Activity:** Help your child learn misspelled words before the final test. Dictate the word and have your child spell the word aloud for you or write it on paper.

Spelling: Vowels in Unstressed Syllables 49

Name_____   **Wilma Unlimited**

Spelling: Vowels in Unstressed Syllables

Word List

different	atmosphere	sentence	communicate	Chicago
register	favorite	instance	gasoline	heavily
carnival	pattern	elegant	factory	garage
variety	understand	aquarium	definite	illustrate

Directions: Write the words from the box that have two **schwa** sounds each. The **schwa** sound is an indistinct vowel sound heard in unstressed syllables, such as the **a** in g<u>a</u>rage or the **o** in fav<u>o</u>rite. Use a dictionary to check your answers.

1. _____   5. _____
2. _____   6. _____
3. _____   7. _____
4. _____

Directions: Choose the word from the box that best completes each equation. Write the word on the line.

8. favor + ite = _____
9. Chicken − ken + ago = _____
10. facts − s + ory = _____
11. heavy − y + ill − l + y = _____
12. patriot − riot + tern = _____
13. sensational − sational + tence = _____
14. il + lustre − e + ate = _____
15. garble − ble + age = _____
16. ga + solo − o + ine = _____
17. define − e + ite = _____
18. under + stand = _____
19. at + most − st + sphere = _____
20. in + stand − d + ce = _____

Notes for Home: Your child spelled words with indistinct vowel sounds that give no clue to their spelling, such as the *i* in *register*. **Home Activity:** Say each word aloud and have your child write it. Review the list and correct any misspellings together.

50 **Spelling: Vowels in Unstressed Syllables**

Wilma Unlimited

Spelling: Vowels in Unstressed Syllables

Directions: Proofread this fan letter. Find seven spelling mistakes. Use the proofreading marks to correct each mistake.

≡	Make a capital.
/	Make a small letter.
∧	Add something.
⌇	Take out something.
⊙	Add a period.
¶	Begin a new paragraph.

Dear Carl Lewis,

I undrstand that you are retiring from competition. Your absence will weigh hevily on this track and field fan!

You are my faverite athlete of all time. The varaty of diffrent events in which you competed was amazing. They all illustrate your great skill. You changed the whole atmusphere of the field when you walked onto it. You had the most elagant running style, and the pattern of exercise and hard work you followed was a great example to me.

With deepest admiration,

Jesse King

Spelling Tip
All the spelling words contain one or more **schwa** sounds, the indistinct vowel sound you hear in unstressed syllables. This vowel sound gives no clues to its spelling, so you need to check these words carefully.

Word List
different
register
carnival
variety
atmosphere
favorite
pattern
understand
sentence
instance
elegant
aquarium
communicate
gasoline
factory
definite
Chicago
heavily
garage
illustrate

Proofread and Write

Write a Fan Letter
On a separate sheet of paper, write a fan letter to an athlete you admire. Try to use at least five of your spelling words.

Notes for Home: Your child spelled words with indistinct vowel sounds that give no clue to their spelling, such as the *i* in *register*. **Home Activity:** Help your child create spelling clues. For example: *Sentence always has three e's.*

Spelling: Vowels in Unstressed Syllables 51

Wilma Unlimited

Spelling: Vowels in Unstressed Syllables

REVIEW

Directions: Choose the word from the box that best matches each clue. Write the word on the line.

Word List
different
register
carnival
variety
atmosphere
favorite
pattern
understand
sentence
instance
elegant
aquarium
communicate
gasoline
factory
definite
Chicago
heavily
garage
illustrate

_____ 1. what someone likes best

_____ 2. certain; positive

_____ 3. tasteful; well-dressed; handsome

_____ 4. with weight

_____ 5. festival; fair

_____ 6. sign up for; record one's name

_____ 7. an example or a case

_____ 8. mass of gases surrounding a star or planet

_____ 9. convey your thoughts or ideas to someone else

_____ 10. a regular order or design

_____ 11. a group of different things

_____ 12. comprehend; grasp the meaning of

Directions: Choose the word from the box that best completes each statement. Write the word on the line to the left.

_____ 13. *Horse* is to *stable* as *car* is to _____.

_____ 14. *Bakers* are to *bakery* as *workers* are to _____.

_____ 15. *Letters* are to *word* as *words* are to _____.

_____ 16. *Human* is to *food* as *motor vehicle* is to _____.

_____ 17. *State* is to *Illinois* as *city* is to _____.

_____ 18. *Bird* is to *cage* as *fish* is to _____.

_____ 19. *Top* is to *bottom* as *alike* is to _____.

_____ 20. *Leap* is to *jump* as *draw* is to _____.

Notes for Home: Your child spelled words with indistinct vowel sounds that give no clue to their spelling, such as the *i* in *register* and the *o* in *atmosphere*. **Home Activity:** Read some of the spelling words aloud. Challenge your child to spell the words.

Name_____ Casey at the Bat

Spelling: Vowels in Final Syllables

Pretest Directions: Fold back the page along the dotted line. On the blanks, write the spelling words as they are dictated. When you have finished the test, unfold the page and check your words.

1. _____
2. _____
3. _____
4. _____
5. _____
6. _____
7. _____
8. _____
9. _____
10. _____
11. _____
12. _____
13. _____
14. _____
15. _____
16. _____
17. _____
18. _____
19. _____
20. _____

1. The store needed a new **slogan**.
2. The immigrant became a **citizen**.
3. **Urban** life can be exciting.
4. Wars **orphan** many children.
5. Have you **forgotten** something?
6. My father teaches **kindergarten**.
7. The plane's **propeller** is stuck.
8. It was a chance **encounter**.
9. Love can **conquer** hate.
10. Would you like an **appetizer**?
11. He is quite a **collector** of junk.
12. The mayor resigned in **dishonor**.
13. The farmer bought a new **tractor**.
14. A tornado can **level** a house.
15. We drove through a long **tunnel**.
16. The painter set up her **easel**.
17. I hit a **double** and a home run.
18. A spider hung by a **single** thread.
19. Can you give me an **example**?
20. We should **recycle** these cans.

Notes for Home: Your child took a pretest on words whose final syllables contain vowels that sound alike but may be spelled differently. *Home Activity:* Have your child divide misspelled words into parts (such as syllables) and concentrate on each part.

Spelling: Vowels in Final Syllables 53

Name _____   **Casey at the Bat**

Spelling: Vowels in Final Syllables

Word List

slogan	forgotten	conquer	tractor	double
urban	kindergarten	appetizer	level	single
orphan	propeller	collector	tunnel	example
citizen	encounter	dishonor	easel	recycle

Directions: Choose the words from the box that end in **-en, -er, -an,** or **-or.**
Listen for the vowels in the final syllables. Write each word in the correct column.

Words Ending -en

1. _____
2. _____
3. _____

Words Ending -an

4. _____
5. _____
6. _____

Words Ending -er

7. _____
8. _____
9. _____
10. _____

Words Ending -or

11. _____
12. _____
13. _____

Directions: Find seven words from the box in the puzzle. They may be printed across or down. Circle the words in the puzzle and then write them on the lines.
Hint: Their final syllables are spelled either **le** or **el**.

14. _____
15. _____
16. _____
17. _____
18. _____
19. _____
20. _____

```
E T U N N E L S
A E L E V X E I
S O U C R A V N
E R A D O M R G
L E V E L P E L
R E C Y C L E E
D O U B L E L D
```

Notes for Home: Your child spelled words whose final syllables contain vowels that often sound alike even when they are spelled differently, such as *slogan* and *citizen*. **Home Activity:** Challenge your child to think of two rhyming words, one ending in *-en* and one ending in *-an*.

54 Spelling: Vowels in Final Syllables

Name _____   Casey at the Bat

Spelling: Vowels in Final Syllables

Directions: Proofread this sports report. Find six spelling mistakes. Use the proofreading marks to correct each mistake.

SPORTS

Today in local baseball, *The Urban Herald Rockets* will encounter its rival newspaper, *The Caspar Citizan Jets*. *The Urben Herald* team has not forgottan last month's single-run loss to *The Caspar Citizen,* in which a 9th inning doubel brought in the winning run. Their slogen for today's match is "Conquor *The Caspar Citizen.*" Fans should make an effort to see a good example of baseball at its best.

≡	Make a capital.
/	Make a small letter.
∧	Add something.
ꭤ	Take out something.
⊙	Add a period.
¶	Begin a new paragraph.

Word List
slogan
urban
orphan
citizen
forgotten
kindergarten
propeller
encounter
conquer
appetizer
collector
dishonor
tractor
level
tunnel
easel
double
single
example
recycle

Spelling Tip
Vowels in final syllables often sound alike even when they are spelled differently: **slog<u>an</u>, citiz<u>en</u>**; **propell<u>er</u>, collect<u>or</u>; lev<u>el</u>, doub<u>le</u>.** Check the sports report carefully to be sure words with these endings are spelled correctly.

Write a Sports Report
On a separate sheet of paper, write your own sports report. Write about an event that has just happened or is just about to happen. Try to use at least five of your spelling words.

Notes for Home: Your child spelled words whose final syllables contain vowels that often sound alike even when they are spelled differently, such as in *slogan* and *citizen*. **Home Activity:** Have your child listen to or read a short sports report and identify words with *-er* and *-or* endings.

Spelling: Vowels in Final Syllables   55

Name _____   **Casey at the Bat**

Spelling: Vowels in Final Syllables   **REVIEW**

Word List
slogan	forgotten	conquer	tractor	double
urban	kindergarten	appetizer	level	single
orphan	propeller	collector	tunnel	example
citizen	encounter	dishonor	easel	recycle

Directions: Choose the word from the box that best matches each clue. Write the word on the line.

_____ 1. This spins around on the front of the airplane.

_____ 2. This is the grade that most five-year-olds are in.

_____ 3. This is what you do when you return bottles for reuse.

_____ 4. This is what a painter uses to support her canvas.

_____ 5. This is an underground passage.

_____ 6. This is what happens when something is not remembered.

_____ 7. This vehicle can pull other farm machinery.

_____ 8. This is the saying an advertiser repeats in commercials.

_____ 9. This is a person who saves certain items, like stamps.

_____ 10. This is a person who has lost his or her parents.

Directions: Choose the word from the box that best replaces the underlined word. Write the word on the line.

_____ 11. The shelf is <u>flat</u> in all directions.

_____ 12. I wouldn't want to <u>meet</u> a bear in the woods.

_____ 13. She is the <u>city</u> planner.

_____ 14. The <u>snack</u> was served just before the entrée.

_____ 15. His shameful actions brought <u>disgrace</u> to his family.

_____ 16. She expects to <u>overcome</u> her fear of flying.

_____ 17. My savings are <u>twice</u> what they were last year.

_____ 18. She showed me a <u>sample</u> of her work.

_____ 19. He is a <u>native</u> of Canada.

_____ 20. The <u>one</u> red pillow was lost in a sea of blue ones.

Notes for Home: Your child spelled words whose final syllables contain vowels that often sound alike even when they are spelled differently, such as *slogan* and *citizen*. **Home Activity:** Challenge your child to spell other words that end with *el* and *le*.

56 Spelling: Vowels in Final Syllables

Name_____ **The Night of the Pomegranate**

Spelling: Homophones

Pretest Directions: Fold back the page along the dotted line. On the blanks, write the spelling words as they are dictated. When you have finished the test, unfold the page and check your words.

1._____	1. **Their** mother is a surgeon.
2._____	2. Put the groceries over **there**.
3._____	3. **They're** not coming until later.
4._____	4. I had to **wring** out my wet shirt.
5._____	5. She has a lovely diamond **ring**.
6._____	6. Please buy some **chili** pepper.
7._____	7. The wind is **chilly** tonight.
8._____	8. That cheese has a strong **scent**.
9._____	9. I **sent** a letter to my uncle.
10._____	10. I don't have a **cent** to my name.
11._____	11. Dad **oversees** our business.
12._____	12. My brother lives **overseas**.
13._____	13. My doctor sees many **patients**.
14._____	14. He has great **patience** with kids.
15._____	15. Open another box of **cereal**.
16._____	16. A **serial** is broadcast in parts.
17._____	17. This wood has a **coarse** grain.
18._____	18. I work at a local golf **course**.
19._____	19. To **counsel** is to give advice.
20._____	20. The city **council** meets today.

Notes for Home: Your child took a pretest on homophones, words that sound alike but are spelled differently and have different meanings. *Home Activity:* Help your child learn to connect the spelling of the word with its meaning.

Spelling: Homophones 57

Name _____   The Night of the Pomegranate

Spelling: Homophones

Word List

their	chili	oversees	cereal	counsel
there	chilly	overseas	serial	council
they're	scent	patients	coarse	
wring	sent	patience	course	
ring	cent			

Directions: Each word below is contained in words from the box. Write the words from the box in the correct column.

over
1. _____
2. _____

tie
3. _____
4. _____

in
5. _____
6. _____

the
7. _____
8. _____
9. _____

Directions: Choose the word from the box that has the same or nearly the same meaning as each word or words below. Write the word on the line.

10. cold _____
11. rough _____
12. committee _____
13. smell _____
14. penny _____
15. breakfast food _____
16. track _____
17. advice _____
18. transmitted _____
19. hot pepper _____
20. in order _____

Notes for Home: Your child spelled homophones—words that sound the same but have different spellings and meanings. **Home Activity:** Help your child write sentences using each spelling word. You may wish to use a dictionary to review the meanings of the words first.

58 Spelling: Homophones

Name _____

The Night of the Pomegranate

Spelling: Homophones

Directions: Proofread this description of the solar system. Find six spelling mistakes. Use the proofreading marks to correct each mistake.

≡	Make a capital.
/	Make a small letter.
∧	Add something.
⌐	Take out something.
⊙	Add a period.
¶	Begin a new paragraph.

I see the solar system as a counsel headed by the Sun. The Sun overseas the planets and guides their course through the chili emptiness of space. Belts of rocks and other debris wring some planets, like Saturn. Their are comets that sometimes outshine the stars. You must have patience if you want to see them, because they are rarely visible. The asteroids that orbit in there belt between Mars and Jupiter are most mysterious to me.

Spelling Tip

their   there

Because homophones sound alike, they are sometimes written incorrectly. **Their** and **there** are often mixed up. Remember **there** refers to a place and think: I looked for it <u>here</u>, but I found it <u>there</u>.

Word List

their	oversees
there	overseas
they're	patients
wring	patience
ring	cereal
chili	serial
chilly	coarse
scent	course
sent	counsel
cent	council

Write a Description

On a separate sheet of paper, write a description of the solar system. It can be a description of what you see in the night sky or what you imagine the surface of a planet would be like. Try to use at least five of your spelling words.

Notes for Home: Your child spelled homophones—words that sound the same but have different spellings and meanings. *Home Activity:* Begin a list of homophones, and work together to keep adding to it with examples such as *to/too/two* or *threw/through*.

Spelling: Homophones 59

Name _____

The Night of the Pomegranate

Spelling: Homophones

REVIEW

Word List

their	chili	oversees	cereal	counsel
there	chilly	overseas	serial	council
they're	scent	patients	coarse	
wring	sent	patience	course	
ring	cent			

Directions: Write the word from the box that belongs in each group.

1. chronological, alphabetical, _____
2. his, her, _____
3. doctors, nurses, _____
4. cold, cool, _____
5. senate, cabinet, _____
6. here, everywhere, _____
7. dime, nickel, _____
8. squeeze, twist, _____
9. mailed, posted, _____
10. he's, she's, _____

Directions: Complete each comparison with a word from the box. Write the word on the line.

_____ 11. The spices in this _____ are as hot as the desert.

_____ 12. The cat's tongue feels as _____ as sandpaper.

_____ 13. The milk has made this _____ as soggy as a swamp.

_____ 14. The delays have everyone's _____ as thin as ice.

_____ 15. The perfume's _____ is like apple blossoms in spring.

_____ 16. The greens on this golf _____ are as smooth as glass.

_____ 17. Patricia _____ her workers as a director does his crew.

_____ 18. His trip _____ on the cruise ship was an adventure.

_____ 19. Her _____ on what to do is as wise as an owl's.

_____ 20. The _____ on her finger sparkled like a star.

Notes for Home: Your child spelled homophones—words that sound the same but have different spellings and meanings. **Home Activity:** Ask your child to write a sentence using the homophones *pair* and *pear*. Repeat with other pairs of homophones.

Name_____ Spring Paint

Spelling: Using Just Enough Letters

Pretest Directions: Fold back the page along the dotted line. On the blanks, write the spelling words as they are dictated. When you have finished the test, unfold the page and check your words.

1. _____
2. _____
3. _____
4. _____
5. _____
6. _____
7. _____
8. _____
9. _____
10. _____
11. _____
12. _____
13. _____
14. _____
15. _____
16. _____
17. _____
18. _____
19. _____
20. _____

1. They have **similar** appearances.
2. Why **doesn't** it snow in July?
3. We often learn by **experience**.
4. **Forward**, march!
5. That is **exactly** what I mean.
6. She is my dancing **partner**.
7. Put your socks in the **drawer**.
8. Lobster is an **expensive** dish.
9. Plants **develop** from seeds.
10. His face is **familiar**.
11. A **pigeon** landed on the statue.
12. Dust is **tickling** my nose.
13. Cheaters face a harsh **penalty**.
14. Rain **frustrated** our picnic plans.
15. She is very **athletic**.
16. This calls for a **celebration**.
17. Birds were **circling** overhead.
18. We rode in a **helicopter**.
19. He is **trembling** from the cold.
20. The stars are **sparkling** tonight.

Pretest

Notes for Home: Your child took a pretest on words with difficult letter combinations.
Home Activity: Help your child learn misspelled words before the final test. Your child should look at the word, say it, spell it aloud, and then spell it with eyes shut.

Spelling: Using Just Enough Letters   **61**

Name_____   Spring Paint

Spelling: Using Just Enough Letters

Think and Practice

Word List				
similar	exactly	develop	penalty	circling
doesn't	partner	familiar	frustrated	helicopter
experience	drawer	pigeon	athletic	trembling
forward	expensive	tickling	celebration	sparkling

Directions: Choose the words from the box that have three or four syllables. Write each word in the correct column.

Words with Three Syllables

1. _____
2. _____
3. _____
4. _____
5. _____
6. _____
7. _____
8. _____

Words with Four Syllables

9. _____
10. _____
11. _____

Directions: Choose the word from the box that best matches each clue. Write the word on the line.

_____ 12. I am the opposite of *backward*.

_____ 13. I am the feeling you get in your nose when you are surrounded by dusty air or fuzzy sweaters.

_____ 14. I am a contraction of the words *does* and *not*.

_____ 15. I am a person you work with or dance with.

_____ 16. I am a gray, black, and white city bird that coos.

_____ 17. I am the part of a desk or chest in which you keep things.

_____ 18. I am similar in meaning to *shaking*.

_____ 19. I am dazzling and shining in the light.

_____ 20. I am an action that will cause you to get dizzy if you do it too often or too fast.

Notes for Home: Your child spelled words that are often misspelled by adding too many letters. *Home Activity:* Write each spelling word on a card. Show your child a card for ten seconds. Have your child pronounce the word carefully, picture how it looks, and spell it aloud.

62 Spelling: Using Just Enough Letters

Name _____   Spring Paint

Spelling: Using Just Enough Letters

Directions: Proofread this description of the Abenaki, a Native American people. Find six spelling mistakes. Use the proofreading marks to correct each mistake.

≡	Make a capital.
/	Make a small letter.
∧	Add something.
⌖	Take out something.
⊙	Add a period.
¶	Begin a new paragraph.

The Abenaki lived in the Northeast, in what is now Vermont and Connecticut. Their lives followed a familare seasonal pattern. They stalked game, raised and harvested crops, fished, and hunted waterfowl and pigeon. Close-knit family groups moved often, so they had to devellop movable homes called *wigwams*. While their experientce was gained through hard living, they had fun too. When the Abenaki held a feast or cellebration, the athtletic men played a game called *lacrosse*. In winter the children played in the sparkeling snow.

Spelling Tip
Pronouncing a word correctly and picturing how it looks can help you avoid writing too many letters. Check the description to make sure the words from the box are spelled correctly.

Word List

similar	pigeon
doesn't	tickling
experience	penalty
forward	frustrated
exactly	athletic
partner	celebration
drawer	circling
expensive	helicopter
develop	trembling
familiar	sparkling

Write a Description
On a separate sheet of paper, write a description of your family. Tell about the house you live in, what you do for work and for fun, and what happens when you have a family celebration. Try to use at least five of your spelling words.

Notes for Home: Your child spelled words that are often misspelled by adding too many letters. **Home Activity:** Copy the list of spelling words, but misspell some of them by adding extra letters. Give your child the list and have him or her find and correct the misspelled words.

Name _____   Spring Paint

Spelling: Using Just Enough Letters REVIEW

Directions: Choose the word from the box that best fits each definition. Write the word on the line.

_____ 1. dove-like city bird
_____ 2. alike
_____ 3. punishment
_____ 4. well-known
_____ 5. small aircraft with a propeller
_____ 6. shaking; quaking
_____ 7. ahead
_____ 8. something you have done or lived through
_____ 9. going around
_____ 10. grow and change

Word List	
similar	pigeon
doesn't	tickling
experience	penalty
forward	frustrated
exactly	athletic
partner	celebration
drawer	circling
expensive	helicopter
develop	trembling
familiar	sparkling

Directions: Choose the word from the box that is the correct form of each word in ( ) to complete each sentence. Write the word on the matching numbered line to the right.

"It **11.** (do not) seem to me that they'll want an **12.** (expense) gift," said Mom. "A family treasure would mean a lot more to your grandparents, since this is their fiftieth anniversary **13.** (celebrate)." We were soon **14.** (frustrate) from wondering **15.** (exact) what would be the ideal gift. Then we looked in the attic, sneezing as its dusty air began **16.** (tickle) our noses. In a **17.** (draw) of the big chest, Mom found an old photo of an **18.** (athlete) Gramps and pretty young Grammie with her **19.** (sparkle) smile. The picture showed each **20.** (part) ready to start a fifty-year journey together. It was perfect.

11. _____
12. _____
13. _____
14. _____
15. _____
16. _____
17. _____
18. _____
19. _____
20. _____

Notes for Home: Your child spelled words that are often misspelled by adding too many letters. **Home Activity:** Take turns with your child using each spelling word in a sentence. Then challenge each other to try to use two or more words in each sentence.

Name _____

A Brother's Promise

Spelling: Including All the Letters

Pretest Directions: Fold back the page along the dotted line. On the blanks, write the spelling words as they are dictated. When you have finished the test, unfold the page and check your words.

1. _____
2. _____
3. _____
4. _____
5. _____
6. _____
7. _____
8. _____
9. _____
10. _____
11. _____
12. _____
13. _____
14. _____
15. _____
16. _____
17. _____
18. _____
19. _____
20. _____

1. There is **probably** enough food.
2. We keep dishes in the **cabinet**.
3. I have a **separate** room.
4. I was just **wondering** why.
5. It is time to wash the **clothes**.
6. What is the **average** test score?
7. He went back to the **beginning**.
8. She opened a new **restaurant**.
9. Do you **promise** to remember?
10. Take some **aspirin** for your pain.
11. It was a **desperate** battle.
12. She was the **twelfth** in line.
13. His brother loves to go **skiing**.
14. There are many **unwritten** rules.
15. It is **roughly** a mile to town.
16. The driver kept to his **schedule**.
17. My parents might **overrule** me.
18. I'm **awfully** sorry for the mistake.
19. How much is this **fishhook**?
20. The **temperature** is dropping.

Pretest

Notes for Home: Your child took a pretest on words with difficult letter combinations. *Home Activity:* Help your child learn misspelled words before the final test. Your child can underline the word parts that caused the problems and concentrate on those parts.

Spelling: Including All the Letters **65**

Name _____   A Brother's Promise

Spelling: Including All the Letters

Word List

probably	temperature	aspirin	skiing
cabinet	average	desperate	unwritten
separate	beginning	awfully	roughly
wondering	restaurant	fishhook	schedule
clothes	promise	twelfth	overrule

Directions: Sort words from the box according to how their endings are spelled. Write each word in the correct column.

Ending in -ing

1. _____
2. _____
3. _____

Ending in -ly

4. _____
5. _____
6. _____

Ending in consonant-vowel-consonant-e

7. _____
8. _____
9. _____
10. _____
11. _____
12. _____
13. _____

Directions: Write the word from the box that belongs in each group.

14. cupboard, chest, _____
15. shoes, hats, _____
16. deli, café, _____
17. vitamin, medicine, _____
18. unspoken, undone, _____
19. tenth, eleventh, _____
20. rod, reel, _____

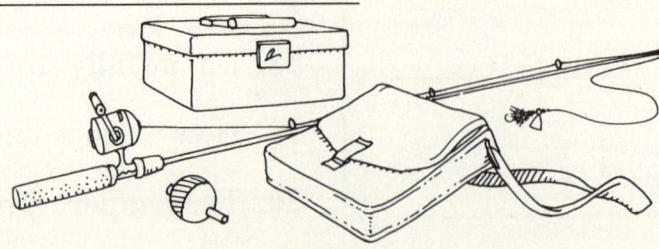

 **Notes for Home:** Your child spelled words with more letters than you might expect. **Home Activity:** Help your child spell these words correctly by pronouncing each syllable carefully or by exaggerating the pronunciation of troublesome letters, such as *prob**a**bly* or *cab**i**net*.

Spelling: Including All the Letters

Directions: Proofread this letter. Find nine spelling mistakes. Use the proofreading marks to correct each mistake.

≡	Make a capital.
/	Make a small letter.
∧	Add something.
⌒	Take out something.
⊙	Add a period.
¶	Begin a new paragraph.

Dear Sophia,

My trip brings me to New York City at the begining of next month, and I will be there until the twelth. That means we'll probibly have time for a real visit. I know rughly what my schedle will be but should have more details soon. Tell me what clothes to bring, as I don't know what the temprature will be. I'm already wondering what fun things we can do. That reminds me of your promis. This time we <u>really must</u> climb the Statue of Liberty. I've been desprate to see the view from her crown.

Love,

Tom

Spelling Tip

All the spelling words have more letters than you might expect. To spell them, pronounce each syllable carefully or exaggerate the pronunciation of troublesome letters. Check the letter to make sure the words from the box are spelled correctly.

Word List

probably	aspirin
cabinet	desperate
separate	awfully
wondering	fishhook
clothes	twelfth
temperature	skiing
average	unwritten
beginning	roughly
restaurant	schedule
promise	overrule

Write a Letter

On a separate sheet of paper, write a letter to a friend, explaining what interests you about a famous tourist attraction. Make plans to visit it together. Try to use at least five of your spelling words.

Notes for Home: Your child spelled words with more letters than you might expect. **Home Activity:** Make up clues or hints about each spelling word, such as *This is something you use to catch a fish.* Challenge your child to guess the word and spell it. *(fishhook)*

Name _____   A Brother's Promise

Spelling: Including All the Letters   REVIEW

Word List

probably	clothes	restaurant	awfully	unwritten
cabinet	temperature	promise	fishhook	roughly
separate	average	aspirin	twelfth	schedule
wondering	beginning	desperate	skiing	overrule

Directions: Choose a word from the box that best matches each clue. Write the word in the puzzle.

Across
1. very likely
3. ordinary; usual
5. medicine to relieve fever or pain
7. opposite of *gently*

Down
2. opposite of *ending*
4. terribly; horribly
6. a winter sport

Directions: Choose a word from the box that best completes each statement. Write the word on the line to the left.

_____ 8. Usher: "Your ticket is for the _____ seat in the third row."

_____ 9. Fisherman: "Bait the _____ carefully."

_____ 10. Carpenter: "How many shelves go in each _____?"

_____ 11. Hungry diner: "Let's eat at the new seafood _____ tonight!"

_____ 12. Weather forecaster: "The _____ is now 90 degrees."

_____ 13. Boss: "The _____ tells you when you'll be working."

_____ 14. Teacher: "Write your answers on a _____ sheet of paper."

_____ 15. Model: "My job is to wear pretty _____ for photographs."

_____ 16. Judge: "I must uphold the law and _____ the objection."

_____ 17. Scientists: "We're _____ what life is like on other planets."

_____ 18. Late children: "We were _____ to get to school on time."

_____ 19. Mother: "The _____ rule is that there is no running in the house!"

_____ 20. Witness: "I must keep my _____ to tell the whole truth."

Notes for Home: Your child spelled words with more letters than you might expect. **Home Activity:** Work with your child to pronounce each word and count its syllables. Write the words and sort them according to the number of syllables in each word.

68   Spelling: Including All the Letters

Name _____ *from* **Catching the Fire**

Spelling: Adding -ed and -ing

Pretest Directions: Fold back the page along the dotted line. On the blanks, write the spelling words as they are dictated. When you have finished the test, unfold the page and check your words.

1. _____
2. _____
3. _____
4. _____
5. _____
6. _____
7. _____
8. _____
9. _____
10. _____
11. _____
12. _____
13. _____
14. _____
15. _____
16. _____
17. _____
18. _____
19. _____
20. _____

1. No one **answered** the telephone.
2. He spent time **answering** them.
3. She **decided** to take a long trip.
4. I'll wait while you're **deciding**.
5. The award **included** money.
6. We all went, **including** Grandma.
7. The essay **omitted** one detail.
8. I hope you are not **omitting** me.
9. The dog's hunger was **satisfied**.
10. I like **satisfying** endings.
11. The slow train **delayed** us.
12. He kept on **delaying** a decision.
13. My mom **remembered** my lunch.
14. I dislike **remembering** that day.
15. She **exercised** for an hour.
16. I love **exercising**.
17. They have **interfered**.
18. Stop **interfering** and help!
19. A great event just **occurred**.
20. The same thing kept **occurring**.

Pretest

Notes for Home: Your child took a pretest on words ending in *-ed* and *-ing*. *Home Activity:* Help your child learn misspelled words before the final test. Have your child learn to spell the base word and then notice how it changes when *-ed* or *-ing* is added.

Spelling: Adding *-ed* and *-ing* **69**

Name _____   *from* **Catching the Fire**

Spelling: Adding -ed and -ing

Word List				
answered	included	satisfied	remembered	interfered
answering	including	satisfying	remembering	interfering
decided	omitted	delayed	exercised	occurred
deciding	omitting	delaying	exercising	occurring

Directions: Choose the words from the box that end in **-ed**. Sort the words according to the way their endings are spelled. Write each word in the correct column.

Just Add -ed

1. _____
2. _____
3. _____

Double the Final Consonant, Then Add -ed

4. _____
5. _____

Drop the Final e, Then Add -ed

6. _____
7. _____
8. _____
9. _____

Directions: Choose the word from the box that best completes each statement. Write the word on the line.

_____ 10. *Smiling* is to *grinning* as *happening* is to _____.

_____ 11. *Queen* is to *ruling* as *busybody* is to _____.

_____ 12. *Love* is to *hating* as *forget* is to _____.

_____ 13. *Try* is to *tried* as *satisfy* is to _____.

_____ 14. *Drawing* is to *sketching* as *replying* is to _____.

_____ 15. *Out* is to *in* as *excluding* is to _____.

_____ 16. *Theater* is to *acting* as *gym* is to _____.

_____ 17. *Early* is to *late* as *hurrying* is to _____.

_____ 18. *On* is to *off* as *enclosing* is to _____.

_____ 19. *Pleasure* is to *pleasing* as *satisfaction* is to _____.

_____ 20. *Pitcher* is to *throwing* as *umpire* is to _____.

Notes for Home: Your child spelled words ending in *-ed* and *-ing*. **Home Activity:** Say the base word for each spelling word, such as *answer* for *answered*. Have your child add *-ed* and *-ing* to each base word and spell the new words he or she has made.

Name _____   *from* **Catching the Fire**

Spelling: Adding -ed and -ing

Directions: Proofread this paragraph that tells of reactions to a quilting class. Find seven spelling mistakes. Use the proofreading marks to correct each mistake.

≡	Make a capital.
/	Make a small letter.
∧	Add something.
⌒	Take out something.
⊙	Add a period.
¶	Begin a new paragraph.

During the first meeting of my quilting class I had trouble rememberring the many techniques presented by the instructor. In the first week of quilting I made several mistakes because I ommitted important steps in the quilting process. It has occured to me that quilting is a difficult and time consuming skill. I am very satisfyed with the beautiful new quilt that I am making, but the completion of the project has been delaied because I don't have enough time to work on it. In fact, I've spent so much time quilting that it has interferred with my homework and the exerciseing that I must do to get into condition for the upcoming basketball season. Quilting is a very old and beautiful craft. Even though it is a lot of work, I am glad that I decided to take the class.

Spelling Tip

The spelling of some base words changes before adding **-ed** or **-ing.** You may need to drop a final **e** as in **decided,** double the final consonant as in **omitting,** or change a final **y** to **i,** as in **satisfied.**

Word List

answered	delayed
answering	delaying
decided	remembered
deciding	remembering
included	exercised
including	exercising
omitted	interfered
omitting	interfering
satisfied	occurred
satisfying	occurring

Write a Paragraph

Find a library book with pictures of quilts and choose one that you like. On a separate sheet of paper, write a paragraph describing the quilt. Try to use at least three of your spelling words.

Notes for Home: Your child spelled words ending in *-ed* and *-ing.* **Home Activity:** Read the Spelling Tip above. Ask your child to identify the spelling words that fall into the three groups described, as well as the spelling words in which the base word does not change.

Name_____   *from* **Catching the Fire**

Spelling: Adding -ed and -ing   REVIEW

		Word List		
answered	included	satisfied	remembered	interfered
answering	including	satisfying	remembering	interfering
decided	omitted	delayed	exercised	occurred
deciding	omitting	delaying	exercising	occurring

Directions: Choose the word from the box that is the most opposite in meaning to each word below. Write the word on the line.

1. forgot _____
2. rushing _____
3. dissatisfied _____
4. avoiding _____
5. including _____
6. undecided _____
7. not happening _____
8. relaxing _____
9. questioning _____
10. leaving out _____

Directions: Choose the word from the box that best replaces the underlined word or words. Write the word on the line.

_____ 11. The quilting instructor <u>responded to</u> my questions about sewing squares of material together.

_____ 12. A lot of beautiful details can be <u>enclosed</u> in a single small section of a quilt.

_____ 13. There is so little room on my four-inch section that some of the fine details were <u>left out</u>.

_____ 14. The elderly quilters passed the hours <u>recalling</u> and telling old stories.

_____ 15. Mary and I <u>stretched</u> after quilting for two hours.

_____ 16. When the instructor demonstrated her skill we all <u>halted</u> our sewing for a while.

_____ 17. Her many careful instructions <u>meddled</u> with our progress in class.

_____ 18. <u>Determining</u> that I had an interest in quilting was easy—finishing a quilt is not easy.

_____ 19. Completing one small portion of the quilt <u>happened</u> very slowly.

_____ 20. It is <u>pleasing</u> to learn a skill that I can teach to my children someday.

Notes for Home: Your child spelled words ending in *-ed* and *-ing*. **Home Activity:** Write all the spelling words that end in *-ed* on separate slips of paper. Take turns drawing words and spelling the words with an *-ing* ending instead of *-ed*.

Name _____

The Seven Wonders of the Ancient World

Spelling: One Consonant or Two?

Pretest Directions: Fold back the page along the dotted line. On the blanks, write the spelling words as they are dictated. When you have finished the test, unfold the page and check your words.

1. _____
2. _____
3. _____
4. _____
5. _____
6. _____
7. _____
8. _____
9. _____
10. _____
11. _____
12. _____
13. _____
14. _____
15. _____
16. _____
17. _____
18. _____
19. _____
20. _____

1. The flights **connect** in Rome.
2. My dog obeys that **command**.
3. How much does the **mirror** cost?
4. Will they **accomplish** their goal?
5. We proceeded **according** to plan.
6. His **allowance** is one dollar.
7. Sonia's sister went to **college**.
8. Print your **address** clearly.
9. The **Mississippi** River flooded.
10. We have **recess** at noon.
11. Our **committee** will plan the trip.
12. What are your **immediate** plans?
13. A **barricade** surrounds the fort.
14. It is impolite to **interrupt**.
15. Lani ate all of her **broccoli**.
16. They **collect** rare stamps.
17. Can you **afford** the movie ticket?
18. They **possess** a lot of land.
19. They drove through **Tennessee**.
20. Who will **announce** the winner?

Pretest

Notes for Home: Your child took a pretest on words that have double consonants. **Home Activity:** Help your child learn misspelled words before the final test. Have your child divide misspelled words into parts (such as syllables) and concentrate on each part.

Spelling: One Consonant or Two? 73

Name _____

The Seven Wonders of the Ancient World

Spelling: One Consonant or Two?

Word List

connect	according	Mississippi	barricade	afford
command	allowance	recess	interrupt	possess
mirror	college	committee	broccoli	Tennessee
accomplish	address	immediate	collect	announce

Directions: Sort the words from the box according to their double consonants. Write the words in the correct column.

The Double Consonants r or c

1. _____
2. _____
3. _____
4. _____
5. _____
6. _____

Two or More Sets of Double Consonants

7. _____
8. _____
9. _____
10. _____
11. _____

Directions: Choose the word from the box that best matches each clue. Write the missing letters of the word in the puzzle.

12. type of school
13. group together
14. right now
15. sum of money paid regularly
16. order
17. have the money to buy
18. school "playtime"
19. make a public statement
20. join together

12. ___ ___ l l ___ ___ ___
13. ___ ___ l l ___ ___ ___
14. ___ m m ___ ___ ___ ___ ___
15. ___ l l ___ ___ ___ ___ ___
16. ___ ___ m m ___ ___ ___
17. ___ f f ___ ___ ___
18. ___ ___ ___ ___ s s
19. ___ n n ___ ___ ___ ___ ___
20. ___ ___ n n ___ ___ ___

Notes for Home: Your child spelled words containing double consonants that stand for only one sound, such as *afford*. **Home Activity:** Scramble the letters for each spelling word. Challenge your child to unscramble them so that the words are spelled correctly.

74 Spelling: One Consonant or Two?

Name _____

The Seven Wonders of the Ancient World

Spelling: One Consonant or Two?

Directions: Proofread this travel brochure. Find five spelling mistakes. Use the proofreading marks to correct each mistake.

≡ Make a capital.
/ Make a small letter.
∧ Add something.
✄ Take out something.
⊙ Add a period.
¶ Begin a new paragraph.

The Travel Comittee of Community Collidge is proud to announce a new tour offering. We call it the Mayan Quest. We'll conect with our tour guides on our journey through several Mayan city-states. The guides will take you through the ruins of pyramids, palaces, and temples. You will see paintings, carvings, and other relics as you discover what the Mayan culture was able to acommplish. This fifteen-day trip is one you cannot afford to miss. An imediate response to our offer is recommended.

Spelling Tip

All the spelling words have double consonants that stand for only one sound, as in a**ff**ord. Try to think of a clue that will help you remember when double consonants are needed. Example: *I can afford to have a second f.*

Word List

connect	committee
command	immediate
mirror	barricade
accomplish	interrupt
according	broccoli
allowance	collect
college	afford
address	possess
Mississippi	Tennessee
recess	announce

Write a Travel Brochure

On a separate sheet of paper, write a travel brochure to encourage people to visit the ruins of an ancient civilization. What will they see there? Why is it important or noteworthy? You may need to do some research before you write. Try to use at least five of your spelling words.

Notes for Home: Your child spelled words containing double consonants that stand for only one sound, such as *afford*. **Home Activity:** Challenge your child to find examples of other words that have two or more sets of double consonants.

Spelling: One Consonant or Two? 75

Name _____

The Seven Wonders of the Ancient World

Spelling: One Consonant or Two?   REVIEW

Word List				
connect	according	Mississippi	barricade	afford
command	allowance	recess	interrupt	possess
mirror	college	committee	broccoli	Tennessee
accomplish	address	immediate	collect	announce

Directions: Write the word from the box that belongs in each group.

1. asparagus, cauliflower, _____
2. order, direct, _____
3. Minnesota, Missouri, _____
4. school, university, _____
5. achieve, finish, _____
6. join, unite, _____
7. instant, now, _____
8. council, group, _____
9. barrier, wall, _____
10. declare, report, _____
11. own, have, _____

Directions: Choose the word from the box that best matches each clue. Write the word on the line.

_____ 12. I am what you can do when you have enough money.

_____ 13. I hang above the sink and show you your face every day.

_____ 14. I contain the cities of Nashville and Memphis.

_____ 15. I am a break for fun during the school day.

_____ 16. I am written on all your mail.

_____ 17. I am what many people do with baseball cards or stamps.

_____ 18. I mean "to break into someone else's speech or actions."

_____ 19. I contain the word *cord*.

_____ 20. I am a sum of money given regularly to someone.

Notes for Home: Your child spelled words containing double consonants that stand for only one sound. **Home Activity:** List the spelling words, making some double consonants single and some single consonants double. Challenge your child to correct the misspellings.

Name_____   The Gold Coin

Spelling: Related Words 1

Pretest Directions: Fold back the page along the dotted line. On the blanks, write the spelling words as they are dictated. When you have finished the test, unfold the page and check your words.

1. _____   1. Language is a **human** trait.
2. _____   2. Treat animals in a **humane** way.
3. _____   3. Please **clean** your room.
4. _____   4. The rain will **cleanse** the street.
5. _____   5. He loved to be out in **nature**.
6. _____   6. She eats only **natural** foods.
7. _____   7. His college **major** was English.
8. _____   8. A **majority** voted for her.
9. _____   9. What is your favorite **poem**?
10. _____   10. Her speech was quite **poetic**.
11. _____   11. We all have **equal** rights.
12. _____   12. Please solve this **equation**.
13. _____   13. **Unite** for the common good.
14. _____   14. Understanding promotes **unity**.
15. _____   15. They diffused the **bomb** in time.
16. _____   16. He'll **bombard** us with questions.
17. _____   17. Exercise builds **muscle**.
18. _____   18. The athlete was very **muscular**.
19. _____   19. As of next week, I hereby **resign**.
20. _____   20. Please hand in your **resignation**.

Notes for Home: Your child took a pretest on related words that have parts spelled the same but pronounced differently. **Home Activity:** Help your child learn misspelled words before the final test by underlining the parts that are different in each pair and concentrating on those.

Spelling: Related Words 1   77

Name_____

The Gold Coin

Spelling: Related Words 1

Word List

human	nature	poem	unite	muscle
humane	natural	poetic	unity	muscular
clean	major	equal	bomb	resign
cleanse	majority	equation	bombard	resignation

Directions: Listen carefully as you read each word from the box aloud. Find the five pairs of related words in which the stressed syllable changes. For example, listen to the difference in stress between **office** and **official**. Write the words on the lines.

Changes in Stressed Syllables

1. _____
2. _____
3. _____
4. _____
5. _____
6. _____
7. _____
8. _____
9. _____
10. _____

Directions: Choose the word from the box that best matches each clue. Write the word on the line.

_____ 11. I am what a shirt is after you wash it.

_____ 12. I am written in verses that may or may not rhyme.

_____ 13. I am a weapon that explodes.

_____ 14. I rhyme with *bends*.

_____ 15. I am how you might describe a strong athlete.

_____ 16. I am what makes you able to clench your fist.

_____ 17. I include all things not made by humans, like forests and oceans.

_____ 18. I am how you might describe a nicely phrased sentence.

_____ 19. I am what children might do to each other with snowballs.

_____ 20. I am the opposite of *artificial*.

Notes for Home: Your child spelled related words that have parts with similar spellings but different pronunciations, such as *human* and *humane*. **Home Activity:** Work with your child to use several spelling words to make a crossword puzzle.

The Gold Coin

Spelling: Related Words 1

Directions: Proofread this "Help Wanted" ad for new storybook characters. Find six spelling mistakes. Use the proofreading marks to correct each mistake.

≡ Make a capital.
/ Make a small letter.
∧ Add something.
⌍ Take out something.
⊙ Add a period.
¶ Begin a new paragraph.

Help Wanted

Due to the resignasion of several characters, new folk tale heroes, villains, and comic sidekicks are needed. Applicants must be able to act in a mature manner. Villains should resign themselves to losing. Heroes must be able to treat all creatures in a humain fashion. A musculler shape is not necessary, but a clean face is required. The ability to use poetac language is a definite plus, especially for princes and knights! Equell opportunities will be given to all applicants, animal or humen. Come join our team!

Spelling Tip
Related words like *resign* and *resignation* have parts that are spelled the same but pronounced differently. Pronounce each word carefully to spell it correctly. Note that the **g** in **resign** is not silent when a suffix is added to form **resignation.**

Word List
human	equal
humane	equation
clean	unite
cleanse	unity
nature	bomb
natural	bombard
major	muscle
majority	muscular
poem	resign
poetic	resignation

Write an Advertisement
On a separate sheet of paper, write an advertisement to find a replacement for a favorite book or movie character. Describe the qualities the applicant needs in order to fill the position. Try to use at least five of your spelling words.

Notes for Home: Your child spelled related words that have parts with similar spellings but different pronunciations, such as *human* and *humane*. **Home Activity:** Play a board game. Make the new rule that before moving, a player must spell a word from the box correctly.

Name _____   The Gold Coin

Spelling: Related Words 1   REVIEW

Word List				
human	nature	poem	unite	muscle
humane	natural	poetic	unity	muscular
clean	major	equal	bomb	resign
cleanse	majority	equation	bombard	resignation

Directions: Choose the word from the box that best completes each statement. Write the word on the line to the left.

_____ 1. *Breathe* is to *lung* as *move* is to _____.

_____ 2. *Fake* is to *real* as *artificial* is to _____.

_____ 3. *Blast* is to *dynamite* as *explosion* is to _____.

_____ 4. *Weak* is to *flabby* as *powerful* is to _____.

_____ 5. *Cruel* is to *kind* as *merciless* is to _____.

_____ 6. *Messy* is to *dirty* as *neat* is to _____.

_____ 7. *Separate* is to *join* as *divide* is to _____.

_____ 8. *Stanza* is to *song* as *verse* is to _____.

_____ 9. *English* is to *sentence* as *mathematics* is to _____.

_____ 10. *Mechanic* is to *car* as *doctor* is to _____.

_____ 11. *Small* is to *large* as *minor* is to _____.

Directions: Choose the word from the box that best replaces the underlined words. Write the word on the line.

_____ 12. Glenda told the Villains' Committee that she would <u>quit</u>.

_____ 13. She gave them her <u>written notice of quitting</u>.

_____ 14. She made a speech laced with <u>vivid, flowing</u> language.

_____ 15. Glenda was tired of struggling against <u>all the forces at work in the world</u>.

_____ 16. People would <u>heavily attack</u> her for her wicked deeds.

_____ 17. Glenda wanted to <u>make clean</u> herself of all evil.

_____ 18. She wanted to give <u>the same</u> time to doing good.

_____ 19. The <u>largest part</u> of the Committee agreed to let her go.

_____ 20. In a rare show of <u>togetherness</u>, the Committee agreed on a replacement.

Notes for Home: Your child spelled related words that have parts with similar spellings but different pronunciations. **Home Activity:** Challenge your child to find and spell a third word that relates to each pair of words on the list, such as *humane, human, humanity*.

Name_____

To the Pole

Spelling: Negative Prefixes

Pretest Directions: Fold back the page along the dotted line. On the blanks, write the spelling words as they are dictated. When you have finished the test, unfold the page and check your words.

1. _____
2. _____
3. _____
4. _____
5. _____
6. _____
7. _____
8. _____
9. _____
10. _____
11. _____
12. _____
13. _____
14. _____
15. _____
16. _____
17. _____
18. _____
19. _____
20. _____

1. I've never done anything **illegal**.
2. Your conclusion is **illogical**.
3. Ink stains left my note **illegible**.
4. The watch is very **inexpensive**.
5. Rumors are often **inaccurate**.
6. He gave an **indirect** answer.
7. It was an **informal** gathering.
8. Don't pretend to be **incapable**.
9. A tornado's power is **incredible**.
10. It is **impolite** to stare at people.
11. That was an **improper** remark.
12. A crack made the cup **imperfect**.
13. I'm **impatient** with my little sister.
14. I have an **imbalance** in my diet.
15. His tantrum was quite **immature**.
16. His actions were **irresponsible**.
17. He has an **irregular** heartbeat.
18. His **irrational** thinking worries me.
19. The puppy is simply **irresistible**.
20. An heirloom is **irreplaceable**.

Pretest

Notes for Home: Your child took a pretest on words with the negative prefixes *il-*, *in-*, *im-*, and *ir-*. **Home Activity:** Help your child learn misspelled words. Your child should look at the word, notice its prefix, say it, spell it aloud, and then spell it with eyes shut.

Spelling: Negative Prefixes 81

Name _____   To the Pole

Spelling: Negative Prefixes

Word List

illegal	inaccurate	incredible	impatient	irregular
illogical	indirect	impolite	imbalance	irrational
illegible	informal	improper	immature	irresistible
inexpensive	incapable	imperfect	irresponsible	irreplaceable

Directions: Choose the word from the box that is formed by adding **il-** or **in-** to each word. Write the word on the line.

1. formal _____
2. logical _____
3. accurate _____
4. direct _____
5. legible _____
6. expensive _____
7. capable _____
8. legal _____
9. credible _____

Directions: Choose the word from the box that best matches each clue. Use each word only once. Write the word on the line.

_____ 10. I am how you feel when you are in a hurry and have to wait.

_____ 11. I am something hard to resist.

_____ 12. I am the kind of behavior that is considered not proper.

_____ 13. I am the kind of spelling word that doesn't follow a rule.

_____ 14. I am the kind of person who does not act like an adult.

_____ 15. I am the kind of person who you do not trust to do an important task.

_____ 16. I am the result when one side is heavier than the other.

_____ 17. I am how you behave when you aren't thinking clearly.

_____ 18. I am not ideal; I have flaws.

_____ 19. I am something or someone that is unique.

_____ 20. I am how you describe a person who has bad manners.

Notes for Home: Your child spelled words with the negative prefixes *il-, in-, im-,* and *ir-*.
Home Activity: Have your child add the prefix *in-* to *effective* and *frequent* and use each word in a sentence. Discuss how adding this prefix changes the meaning of words.

Name _____   **To the Pole**

Spelling: Negative Prefixes

Directions: Proofread this letter from an Arctic expedition. Find seven spelling mistakes. Use the proofreading marks to correct each mistake.

≡	Make a capital.
/	Make a small letter.
∧	Add something.
ꝰ	Take out something.
⊙	Add a period.
¶	Begin a new paragraph.

Dear Dad,

   If this letter ever reaches you, it will be by a very undirect route, but the temptation to try is iresistible. We're stuck in a settlement that has iregular contact with the outside world, so any prediction of when my letter can go is bound to be innaccurate.

   The Arctic is incredible—I'm imcapable of finding words for it! I feel an unlogical impulse to speak in a whisper—I'm almost afraid to break the vast silence of the landscape. Maybe twenty-four hours of daylight has made me irrational.

   If my writing is illegible, it's Ben's fault—he is inpatient to go exploring. We are both well and eager to see you and Mom soon.

                                    Love,
                                    Marianne

Proofread and Write

Spelling Tip
When negative prefixes are added to base words, the spelling of the base word does not change. Check the letter to make sure the beginnings of words are spelled correctly.

Word List
illegal	improper
illogical	imperfect
illegible	impatient
inexpensive	imbalance
inaccurate	immature
indirect	irresponsible
informal	irregular
incapable	irrational
incredible	irresistible
impolite	irreplaceable

Write a Letter
On a separate sheet of paper, write a letter to Marianne from her father. Try to use at least three spelling words.

Notes for Home: Your child spelled words with the negative prefixes *il-*, *in-*, *im-*, and *ir-*.
Home Activity: Give your child the base word for each spelling word. Have him or her add one of the negative prefixes to each base word to form a spelling word *(il + legal = illegal).*

Spelling: Negative Prefixes   83

Name_____   To the Pole

Spelling: Negative Prefixes   REVIEW

Word List

illegal	inaccurate	incredible	impatient	irregular
illogical	indirect	impolite	imbalance	irrational
illegible	informal	improper	immature	irresistible
inexpensive	incapable	imperfect	irresponsible	irreplaceable

Directions: Choose the word from the box that is the negative form of the word in parentheses and that makes sense in the sentence. Write the word on the line.

_____ 1. I am (patient) to begin the trip north to the Arctic.

_____ 2. Arctic travel is (logical) without careful planning.

_____ 3. You can freeze to death if you wear (proper) clothing.

_____ 4. Going alone would be (regular); groups are safer.

_____ 5. (Responsible) people could endanger the whole group.

_____ 6. That means we can't take Celia; she is too (mature).

_____ 7. Celia can't overcome her (rational) fear of snow.

_____ 8. An (direct) route will take longer, but we will see more.

_____ 9. The (balance) of the load on the sled will make it tip over.

_____ 10. We all enjoy our (formal) dinners around the campfire.

Directions: Choose the word from the box that best matches each definition. Write the word on the line.

_____ 11. unique; impossible to replace

_____ 12. flawed or defective

_____ 13. ill-mannered; rude

_____ 14. cheap; easily affordable

_____ 15. against the law

_____ 16. overwhelming; strongly tempting

_____ 17. without ability

_____ 18. difficult or impossible to read

_____ 19. containing mistakes; not exact

_____ 20. hard to believe; extraordinary

Notes for Home: Your child spelled words with the negative prefixes *il-, in-, im-,* and *ir-*.
Home Activity: Write the four negative prefixes on separate sheets of paper. Say each spelling word aloud and have your child write the word on the correct sheet.

Name _____   *from* El Güero

Spelling: Suffixes -ation, -tion, -ion

Pretest Directions: Fold back the page along the dotted line. On the blanks, write the spelling words as they are dictated. When you have finished the test, unfold the page and check your words.

1. _____
2. _____
3. _____
4. _____
5. _____
6. _____
7. _____
8. _____
9. _____
10. _____
11. _____
12. _____
13. _____
14. _____
15. _____
16. _____
17. _____
18. _____
19. _____
20. _____

1. **Relaxation** lessens tension.
2. Space **exploration** continues.
3. What is your **occupation**?
4. The train reached its **destination**.
5. New students attend **orientation**.
6. He made the **recommendation**.
7. **Determination** helps success.
8. My cut has a minor **infection**.
9. The **collection** was for the sick.
10. His **reaction** was one of surprise.
11. It was a difficult **situation**.
12. Please turn off the **television**.
13. Ours is a hopeful **generation**.
14. On **reflection**, I'll try it.
15. The forest faces **destruction**.
16. Pay **attention** to the lesson.
17. Use **deduction** to solve it.
18. We held the wedding **reception**.
19. We need a **solution** quickly.
20. The **convention** was at the hotel.

Pretest

Notes for Home: Your child took a pretest on words that have the suffixes *-ation*, *-tion*, and *-ion*. **Home Activity:** Help your child learn misspelled words before the final test. Your child can underline the word parts that caused the problems and concentrate on those parts.

Spelling: Suffixes *-ation, -tion, -ion*

Name _____   *from* El Güero

Spelling: Suffixes -ation, -tion, -ion

Word List

relaxation	recommendation	situation	attention
exploration	determination	television	deduction
occupation	infection	generation	reception
destination	collection	reflection	solution
orientation	reaction	destruction	convention

Directions: Add a suffix to each base word below to form a word from the box. Write the word on the line.

1. determine _____
2. convene _____
3. situate _____
4. generate _____
5. solve _____
6. televise _____
7. attend _____
8. occupy _____
9. deduce _____
10. explore _____
11. receive _____
12. destiny _____

Directions: Choose the word from the box that best completes each equation. Write the word on the line.

13. re + commence – ce + dation = _____
14. destroy – oy + uction = _____
15. re + lax + a + tion = _____
16. reach – h + tion = _____
17. in + fect – t + tion = _____
18. color – or + lec + tion = _____
19. orient + ate – te + tion = _____
20. reflexes – xes + c + tion = _____

Notes for Home: Your child spelled words with the suffixes *-ation*, *-tion*, and *-ion*.
Home Activity: Challenge your child to add the suffix *-ion* to each of these words and use the new words in sentences: *elect, act, construct.*

86 Spelling: Suffixes *-ation, -tion, -ion*

Name _____   *from* El Güero

Spelling: Suffixes -ation, -tion, -ion

Directions: Proofread this humorous account of a canine exile's thoughts. Find six spelling mistakes. Use the proofreading marks to correct each mistake.

≡	Make a capital.
/	Make a small letter.
∧	Add something.
℘	Take out something.
⊙	Add a period.
¶	Begin a new paragraph.

How can I get back in? Is my life of relaxashon in front of the telavision over? I miss the attention and affection of the people inside.

I didn't mean any harm. I was wandering about without a specific destination and decided a little exploreation under the shed would be fun. Who knew a spray in the face would be my recepsion? And now, though I've barked my reccomendation to be allowed in, I'm banned from the house until the skunk smell wears off. I never expected this reaction to my situasion.

Proofread and Write

Spelling Tip

When adding the suffixes **-ation**, **-tion**, or **-ion**, some base words do not change: **relaxation**. Other base words may drop a final **e** or **y**: **exploration, occupation**. Some base words have other changes: **receive + -tion = reception**

Word List

relaxation	situation
exploration	television
occupation	generation
destination	reflection
orientation	destruction
recommendation	attention
determination	deduction
infection	reception
collection	solution
reaction	convention

Write a Narrative

On a separate sheet of paper, write a narrative that describes thoughts that might occupy an exile's mind. It can be humorous, like the dog's tale above, or serious. What does an exile feel? What might an exile do? Try to use at least five spelling words in your narrative.

Notes for Home: Your child spelled words with suffixes *-ation, -tion, -ion*. **Home Activity:** Challenge your child to identify the base word in each word from the box and to tell whether the spelling of the base word changed when the suffix was added.

Spelling: Suffixes *-ation, -tion, -ion* 87

Name _____ *from* El Güero

Spelling: Suffixes -ation, -tion, -ion **REVIEW**

Word List			
relaxation	recommendation	situation	attention
exploration	determination	television	deduction
occupation	infection	generation	reception
destination	collection	reflection	solution
orientation	reaction	destruction	convention

Directions: Choose the word from the box that best completes each sentence. Write the word on the line to the left.

_____ 1. Before school started in the fall, her _____ was being a lifeguard at the local beach.

_____ 2. The train took her straight to her _____: Lowwood School.

_____ 3. Her _____ by the older students was warm and friendly.

_____ 4. They had taken up a _____ to buy party refreshments to make the "new girl in town" feel more at home.

_____ 5. She found a _____ to her isolation in new friendships.

_____ 6. She paid _____ in class, wanting to do well in her studies.

_____ 7. Dinner was a welcome form of _____ after each busy day.

_____ 8. She rarely found time to watch _____ after dinner.

_____ 9. Her _____ to make a better life for herself in this country was admired by many.

_____ 10. Each _____ in her family had always had at least one person eager to try new adventures.

Directions: Choose the word from the box that has the same or nearly the same meaning as each word or words below. Write the word on the line.

11. response _____
12. search _____
13. adjustment _____
14. mirror image _____
15. subtraction _____
16. suggestion _____
17. disease _____
18. conference _____
19. circumstances _____
20. ruin _____

Notes for Home: Your child reviewed words with suffixes *-ation, -ion, -tion*. **Home Activity:** Write the base word of each spelling word on index cards. Have your child pick a card and add a suffix to form a spelling word *(occupy + -tion = occupation)*.

Name_____

Destination: Mars

Spelling: Opposite Prefixes

Pretest Directions: Fold back the page along the dotted line. On the blanks, write the spelling words as they are dictated. When you have finished the test, unfold the page and check your words.

1. _____
2. _____
3. _____
4. _____
5. _____
6. _____
7. _____
8. _____
9. _____
10. _____
11. _____
12. _____
13. _____
14. _____
15. _____
16. _____
17. _____
18. _____
19. _____
20. _____

1. The **pretrial** hearing was short.
2. We will **prearrange** the vacation.
3. The crime was not **premeditated**.
4. She found a **prehistoric** fossil.
5. Proper **precaution** is wise.
6. The houses **postdate** the farm.
7. **Postwar** Europe prospered.
8. The **postponement** is temporary.
9. She did **postgraduate** studies.
10. Do not **overcook** the rice.
11. The cliffs **overlook** the sea.
12. The pot began to **overflow**.
13. The zoo was **overpopulated**.
14. Stay **undercover** until it is safe.
15. The bear looked **undernourished**.
16. The luggage was **underweight**.
17. Does the meal **include** a salad?
18. I like to **inhale** baking smells.
19. Do not **exclude** your friends.
20. They **exhale** audibly.

Pretest

Notes for Home: Your child took a pretest on words with the prefixes *pre-*, *post-*, *over-*, *under-*, *in-*, and *ex-*. **Home Activity:** Help your child learn misspelled words before the final test. Dictate the word and have your child spell the word aloud for you or write it on paper.

Spelling: Opposite Prefixes 89

Name _____   Destination: Mars

Spelling: Opposite Prefixes

Word List				
pretrial	precaution	postgraduate	overpopulated	include
prearrange	postdate	overcook	undercover	inhale
premeditated	postwar	overlook	undernourished	exclude
prehistoric	postponement	overflow	underweight	exhale

Directions: Choose the words from the box that have the prefixes **pre-, post-, in-** or **ex-**. Write each word in the correct column.

Prefix pre-

1. _____
2. _____
3. _____
4. _____
5. _____

Prefix post-

8. _____
9. _____
10. _____
11. _____

Prefix in-

6. _____
7. _____

Prefix ex-

12. _____
13. _____

Directions: Choose the word from the box that matches each definition. Write the word on the line.

_____ 14. cook too much

_____ 15. not heavy enough

_____ 16. not eating a healthful diet

_____ 17. go over or beyond the limits; flood

_____ 18. not to see something

_____ 19. in secret

_____ 20. crowded with people

Notes for Home: Your child spelled words with the prefixes *pre-, post-, over-, under-, in-,* and *ex-*. **Home Activity:** Have your child name two words not on the list that can be formed by adding the prefix *under-* and two words that can be formed by adding the prefix *over-*.

Name_____ Destination: Mars

Spelling: Opposite Prefixes

Directions: Proofread this space log. Find seven spelling mistakes. Use the proofreading marks to correct each mistake.

| = Make a capital.
| / Make a small letter.
| ∧ Add something.
| ℘ Take out something.
| ⊙ Add a period.
| ¶ Begin a new paragraph.

Today we made our first poswar visit to Elkan. After 40 years of isolation, conditions on the planet are, by our standards, perhistoric. Going without is a way of life for this population, which appears undrnourished and underweight.

The purposes of our prarranged meeting included locating a suitable site for pertrial hearings and discussing the charges of premeditated war crimes. I discovered that the former leaders charged with these crimes have taken the preccaution of filing for a trial posponement. I fear this mission will be a long one.

Spelling Tip
When adding the prefixes **pre-, post-, over-, under-, in-,** and **ex-**, do not make any changes in the base word.

Word List
pretrial	overlook
prearrange	overflow
premeditated	overpopulated
prehistoric	undercover
precaution	undernourished
postdate	underweight
postwar	include
postponement	inhale
postgraduate	exclude
overcook	exhale

Write a Space Log Entry
On a separate sheet of paper, write an entry in a space log. What did you do in space today? Were there any problems? Try to use at least five spelling words.

Notes for Home: Your child spelled words with the prefixes *pre-, post-, over-, under-, in-,* and *ex-*. **Home Activity:** Help your child separate the prefixes from the base words in the spelling list *(pretrial = pre + trial)*. Discuss how prefixes change the meaning of base words.

Name_____ Destination: Mars

Spelling: Opposite Prefixes **REVIEW**

Word List				
pretrial	precaution	postgraduate	overpopulated	include
prearrange	postdate	overcook	undercover	inhale
premeditated	postwar	overlook	undernourished	exclude
prehistoric	postponement	overflow	underweight	exhale

Directions: Find two words in each sentence that can be combined to form a word from the box. Write the word from the box on the line.

_____ 1. Put the papers under the brass weight.

_____ 2. I went over to his house to look for him.

_____ 3. That post was destroyed in the war.

_____ 4. If you come over for dinner, I will cook spaghetti.

_____ 5. The post office stamps the date on each letter.

_____ 6. Let's go over to the bridge and watch the river flow.

_____ 7. He left his military post just as his son was about to graduate.

_____ 8. I found a book under the couch; look at the dust on its cover!

_____ 9. We traveled over stretches of country populated by cattle.

_____ 10. Clams live under the water; they are nourished by the sea.

Directions: Choose the word from the box that best answers each riddle. Write the word on the line.

_____ 11. I am what you do when you take in a breath.

_____ 12. I am what you do when you release your breath.

_____ 13. I am from the time before written history.

_____ 14. I am what you ask for if you want to put something off until later.

_____ 15. I am what you do when you make an arrangement in advance.

_____ 16. I am what you do when you make someone part of a group.

_____ 17. I am what you take beforehand to ensure your safety.

_____ 18. I am a meeting before a trial.

_____ 19. I am what you do when you shut something or someone out.

_____ 20. I am a type of action that has been thought out in advance.

Notes for Home: Your child reviewed words with the prefixes *pre-*, *post-*, *over-*, *under-*, *in-*, and *ex-*. **Home Activity:** Write the spelling words on separate index cards. Take turns with your child choosing a card from the stack, spelling the word, and using it in a sentence.

Name_____

The Land of Expectations

Spelling: Suffixes -ate, -ive, -ship

Pretest Directions: Fold back the page along the dotted line. On the blanks, write the spelling words as they are dictated. When you have finished the test, unfold the page and check your words.

1. _____
2. _____
3. _____
4. _____
5. _____
6. _____
7. _____
8. _____
9. _____
10. _____
11. _____
12. _____
13. _____
14. _____
15. _____
16. _____
17. _____
18. _____
19. _____
20. _____

1. Let's **originate** a new recipe.
2. I'm **fortunate** to have friends.
3. Please **activate** my account.
4. Her cat is very **affectionate**.
5. He is kind and **considerate**.
6. Your duties **obligate** you to try.
7. We had a **productive** lesson.
8. This toy is **defective**.
9. Her ideas were **constructive**.
10. He has an **attractive** apartment.
11. She is an **inventive** writer.
12. The insult had a **negative** effect.
13. He is a **creative** painter.
14. I claim **ownership** of this book.
15. The club **membership** is free.
16. Poverty is a terrible **hardship**.
17. What is your **relationship**?
18. We have a solid **friendship**.
19. We will win the **championship**.
20. She has natural **leadership**.

Pretest

Notes for Home: Your child took a pretest on words that have the suffixes *-ate*, *-ive*, and *-ship*. **Home Activity:** Help your child learn misspelled words before the final test. Have your child divide misspelled words into parts (such as syllables) and concentrate on each part.

Spelling: Suffixes *-ate, -ive, -ship* 93

Name _____

The Land of Expectations

Spelling: Suffixes -ate, -ive, -ship

Word List

originate	obligate	inventive	hardship
fortunate	productive	negative	relationship
activate	defective	creative	friendship
affectionate	constructive	ownership	championship
considerate	attractive	membership	leadership

Directions: Choose the words from the box that have the suffixes **-ate** and **-ive**. Write each word in the correct column.

Suffix -ive

1. _____
2. _____
3. _____
4. _____
5. _____
6. _____
7. _____

Suffix -ate

8. _____
9. _____
10. _____
11. _____
12. _____
13. _____

Directions: Choose the word from the box that best answers each riddle. Write the word on the line.

_____ 14. I am a victory in the World Series or the Super Bowl.

_____ 15. I am a synonym of the word *possession*.

_____ 16. I am poverty, sorrow, difficulty, or hunger.

_____ 17. I am the link between any two people who know each other.

_____ 18. I am the link between two people who are friends.

_____ 19. I am a quality generals, presidents, and kings should have.

_____ 20. I am what you apply for if you want to join a club or group.

Notes for Home: Your child spelled words with suffixes *-ate*, *-ive*, and *-ship*. **Home Activity:** Help your child identify the base word of each spelling word. Then discuss whether the spelling of the base word changed when the suffix was added.

Name _____   The Land of Expectations

Spelling: Suffixes -ate, -ive, -ship

Directions: Proofread this transcript of a sports broadcast. Find five spelling mistakes. Use the proofreading marks to correct each mistake.

| ≡ Make a capital. |
| / Make a small letter. |
| ∧ Add something. |
| ⌒ Take out something. |
| ⊙ Add a period. |
| ¶ Begin a new paragraph. |

After five days of long, wet, dark hardship, Jennifer Dizeck can almost see the finish line of the Center of the Earth Championnship. Owneship of the prized cup seems almost certain. But what's this? She is taking on water! Will a defective canoe obligate Jennifer to pull out of the race?

Jennifer seems to be back in control. It is fortunite she is so resourceful. She was inventave enough to plug the hole with her waterproof jacket. That's good, creative thinking on Jennifer's part! She's regained her leadershap position in the last mile of the race. Jennifer Dizeck wins by a few feet!

Spelling Tip
For base words that end in **e**, drop the **e** before adding the suffixes **-ate, -ive,** or **-ship: obligate, creative.**

Word List
originate	inventive
fortunate	negative
activate	creative
affectionate	ownership
considerate	membership
obligate	hardship
productive	relationship
defective	friendship
constructive	championship
attractive	leadership

Write a Sports Broadcast
On a separate sheet of paper, write a sports broadcast about an imaginary new sporting event. Remember that a broadcaster reports the action as he or she watches it happen. Try to use at least three spelling words.

Notes for Home: Your child spelled words with the suffixes *-ate, -ive,* and *-ship.* **Home Activity:** Have your child scan a magazine article to find other words that contain the suffixes *-ate, -ive,* and *-ship.* Encourage him or her to tell you the base word of each of the words.

Spelling: Suffixes *-ate, -ive, -ship* 95

Name _____   The Land of Expectations

Spelling: Suffixes -ate, -ive, -ship   REVIEW

Word List

originate	considerate	constructive	creative	relationship
fortunate	obligate	attractive	ownership	friendship
activate	productive	inventive	membership	championship
affectionate	defective	negative	hardship	leadership

Directions: Write the word from the box that belongs in each group.

1. fellowship, companionship, _____
2. faulty, imperfect, _____
3. disapproving, pessimistic, _____
4. authority, guidance, _____
5. fertile, fruitful, _____
6. begin, start, _____
7. burden, misfortune, _____
8. affiliation, association, _____
9. possession, title, _____
10. loving, cuddly, _____

Directions: Choose the word from the box that best replaces the underlined word or words. Write the word on the line.

_____ 11. My association with time travel began long ago.
_____ 12. In an imaginative mood, I built my own time machine.
_____ 13. My best friend Josh offered helpful criticism.
_____ 14. Josh was ingenious enough to fix the flaws in the machine.
_____ 15. I was very lucky to have a sympathetic friend like him.
_____ 16. Together we had won the victory medal in the science fair.
_____ 17. My voyage will begin here in Kansas City; my destination is Paris in 1899.
_____ 18. The trip sounded appealing to Josh, but he couldn't come.
_____ 19. He did require me to promise that he could go on the next trip.
_____ 20. It was very thoughtful of Josh to see me off.

Notes for Home: Your child reviewed words with the suffixes *-ate, -ive,* and *-ship.* **Home Activity:** Challenge your child to spell *inventive* and *creative,* use each word in a sentence, and explain the similarities and differences between the meanings of the two words.

Name_____   **The Trail Drive**

Spelling: Using Apostrophes

Pretest Directions: Fold back the page along the dotted line. On the blanks, write the spelling words as they are dictated. When you have finished the test, unfold the page and check your words.

1._____	1. **It's** not time to go already, is it?
2._____	2. **Let's** go bowling.
3._____	3. I think **that's** a great idea.
4._____	4. **We'd** rather go to the zoo.
5._____	5. They **don't** know who called.
6._____	6. **There's** a pie for dessert.
7._____	7. The **coach's** hat fell off.
8._____	8. The **coaches'** whistles are loud.
9._____	9. That **man's** pants are plaid.
10._____	10. Those **men's** jobs are all done.
11._____	11. **You're** just the person I need.
12._____	12. **She'd** tell us if she knew.
13._____	13. You **mustn't** stay out too late.
14._____	14. It is after ten **o'clock**.
15._____	15. Our **guide's** walking stick broke.
16._____	16. The **guides'** station is over there.
17._____	17. She sat in the **director's** desk.
18._____	18. The **directors'** offices are locked.
19._____	19. This **city's** mayor is Mr. Jones.
20._____	20. Those **cities'** names are alike.

Pretest

Notes for Home: Your child took a pretest on contractions and possessives with apostrophes. *Home Activity:* Help your child learn misspelled words before the final test by concentrating on which two words are shortened to one or on whether one person or more than one person owns something.

Spelling: Using Apostrophes 97

Name_____   **The Trail Drive**

Spelling: Using Apostrophes

Word List

it's	don't	man's	mustn't	director's
let's	there's	men's	o'clock	directors'
that's	coach's	you're	guide's	city's
we'd	coaches'	she'd	guides'	cities'

Directions: Choose the words from the box that are possessive nouns. Write each word in the correct column.

Singular Possessive Nouns

1. _____
2. _____
3. _____
4. _____
5. _____

Plural Possessive Nouns

6. _____
7. _____
8. _____
9. _____
10. _____

Directions: Choose the word from the box that best replaces each underlined word or words. Write the word on the line.

_____ 11. "It is morning! Time to get up!" called Aunt Carmela.

_____ 12. "Seven A.M. is too early to get up," grumbled Alice.

_____ 13. "On a farm, that is very late," her aunt explained.

_____ 14. "We would never get our work done if we slept that late."

_____ 15. "After you've eaten," said Uncle Tony, "let us go to the barn."

_____ 16. "You are going to learn how to milk, Alice," he explained.

_____ 17. "I do not think I can," objected Alice. "Cows scare me."

_____ 18. "You must not be scared, Alice. They are very gentle."

_____ 19. "Look, Uncle Tony!" cried Alice later. "There is the full pail of milk!"

_____ 20. After this success, Alice knew she would like living on the farm.

Notes for Home: Your child used apostrophes to spell contractions and possessives. *Home Activity:* Challenge your child to tell you the two words each contraction represents. Note that some can stand for different combinations: *she'd = she had, she did,* or *she would.*

98 Spelling: Using Apostrophes

Name _____

The Trail Drive

Spelling: Using Apostrophes

Directions: Proofread this cowboy song. Find five spelling mistakes. Use the proofreading marks to correct each mistake.

| = Make a capital. |
| / Make a small letter. |
| ∧ Add something. |
| ✐ Take out something. |
| ⊙ Add a period. |
| ¶ Begin a new paragraph. |

A citys' lights do'nt mean a thing to me.

That's not where this mans' heart will ever be.

Its the Chisholm Trail that calls.

Let's ride the range, we will see it all.

Theres' joy and laughter when you're riding free.

Spelling Tip

man's men's cities'
To form the possessive of a singular noun or a plural noun that does not end in **s**, add an **apostrophe** and an **s**: **man's, men's.** For plural nouns that end in **s**, just add an apostrophe to form the possessive: **cities'.** Check the cowboy song to be sure the plurals are formed correctly.

Word List

it's	there's	you're	guides'
let's	coach's	she'd	director's
that's	coaches'	mustn't	directors'
we'd	man's	o'clock	city's
don't	men's	guide's	cities'

Write a Song

On a separate sheet of paper, write your own cowboy song. Think about experiences that a cowhand on a ranch might have. Try to use at least five spelling words.

Notes for Home: Your child used apostrophes to spell contractions and possessives. *Home Activity:* Have your child use the spelling words in sentences. Check for the correct use of singular and plural possessives.

Spelling: Using Apostrophes

Name _____

The Trail Drive

Spelling: Using Apostrophes

REVIEW

Word List				
it's	don't	man's	mustn't	director's
let's	there's	men's	o'clock	directors'
that's	coach's	you're	guide's	city's
we'd	coaches'	she'd	guides'	cities'

Directions: Each underlined word is missing its apostrophe. Write each word correctly on the line, inserting the apostrophe in its proper place.

_____ 1. Jud: <u>Theres</u> a fair this Saturday. Would you like to go?

_____ 2. Laurey: I <u>dont</u> know. Where is it going to be held?

_____ 3. Jud: <u>Its</u> near the Simpson ranch.

_____ 4. Laurey: Oh, <u>thats</u> not far. I would like to go!

_____ 5. Jud: It starts at 8 <u>oclock</u>.

_____ 6. Laurey: Well, <u>lets</u> not be late.

_____ 7. Jud: <u>Wed</u> better invite your sister to come along.

_____ 8. Laurey: <u>Shed</u> probably like that.

_____ 9. Jud: We <u>mustnt</u> forget to ask her.

_____ 10. Laurey: <u>Youre</u> coming to dinner tonight. We'll ask her then.

Directions: Complete each phrase with the correct possessive word in ( ). Write the word on the line.

_____ 11. Singular: (director's/directors') chair

_____ 12. Plural: (coach's/coaches') offices

_____ 13. Plural: (guide's/guides') presentations

_____ 14. Singular: (city's/cities') art museum

_____ 15. Plural: (director's/directors') awards

_____ 16. Singular: (coach's/coaches') whistle

_____ 17. Singular: (man's/men's) hat

_____ 18. Singular: (guide's/guides') tour

_____ 19. Plural: (city's/cities') skyscrapers

_____ 20. Plural: (man's/men's) choirs

Notes for Home: Your child used apostrophes to spell contractions and possessives. **Home Activity:** Help your child write sentences that contain both a contraction and a possessive from the word list.

Name_____

Noah Writes a B & B Letter

Spelling: Easily Confused Words

Pretest Directions: Fold back the page along the dotted line. On the blanks, write the spelling words as they are dictated. When you have finished the test, unfold the page and check your words.

1._____   1. It has been raining **since** noon.
2._____   2. That movie made no **sense**.
3._____   3. You must **choose** only one.
4._____   4. He **chose** a vanilla milkshake.
5._____   5. The bus **finally** arrived.
6._____   6. The watch is **finely** engraved.
7._____   7. Everybody went **except** Todd.
8._____   8. We **accept** your apology.
9._____   9. A tree stands **beside** the barn.
10._____ 10. I like all fruit **besides** pears.
11._____ 11. The Internet is a **recent** invention.
12._____ 12. I **resent** your rude comments.
13._____ 13. She needs **access** to those files.
14._____ 14. I have an **excess** of comic books.
15._____ 15. We will meet at home **later**.
16._____ 16. I like the **latter** parts of the play.
17._____ 17. The gate was made of **metal**.
18._____ 18. The soldier earned a **medal**.
19._____ 19. It is a **personal** matter.
20._____ 20. He is in charge of **personnel**.

Notes for Home: Your child took a pretest on words that are easily confused because of similar pronunciations and spellings. *Home Activity:* Help your child learn misspelled words before the final test. Your child should look at the word, say it, spell it aloud, and then spell it with eyes shut.

Spelling: Easily Confused Words 101

Spelling: Easily Confused Words

Word List

since	finally	beside	access	metal
sense	finely	besides	excess	medal
choose	except	recent	later	personal
chose	accept	resent	latter	personnel

Directions: Choose the word from the box that best matches each definition. Write the word on the line.

_____ 1. too much; overflow

_____ 2. right to enter or use

_____ 3. feel injured and angry

_____ 4. not long ago

_____ 5. select

_____ 6. selected

_____ 7. in the end

_____ 8. delicately

_____ 9. next to

_____ 10. other than, in addition to

_____ 11. award; decoration

_____ 12. a substance such as iron, steel, silver, or gold

Directions: Choose the word in ( ) that best completes each sentence. Write the word on the line.

_____ 13. The couple will gladly (except/accept) any wedding presents.

_____ 14. Ever (since/sense) yesterday, guests have been arriving for the wedding.

_____ 15. The (later/latter) of the two flower girls in the procession was taller.

_____ 16. (Except/Accept) for Jill, the bridesmaids were all blonde.

_____ 17. The (personal/personnel) from the church were glad to help.

_____ 18. The groom had the (since/sense) that the bride was nervous.

_____ 19. He knew that (later/latter) in the day she would feel better.

_____ 20. In my (personal/personnel) opinion, it was a lovely wedding.

Notes for Home: Your child spelled words that are easily confused because of similar pronunciations and spellings. *Home Activity:* Write a definition of each spelling word on an index card. Have your child choose a card, spell the word defined, and use it in a sentence.

102 Spelling: Easily Confused Words

Name _____   **Noah Writes a B & B Letter**

Spelling: Easily Confused Words

Directions: Proofread the signs Lynn saw in her grandparents' store. Find six spelling mistakes. Use the proofreading marks to correct each mistake.

Proofreading Marks
≡ Make a capital.
/ Make a small letter.
∧ Add something.
ꟼ Take out something.
⊙ Add a period.
¶ Begin a new paragraph.

Proofread and Write

- All personall are to separate plastic bottles from metal cans and containers.
- It's getting latter by the minute, so get busy!
- Do not except checks without two forms of identification.
- Do not block access to this door.
- Due to resent weather problems, vegetable prices have risen!
- Please dispose of eksess boxes properly.
- The new uniforms you chose last month have finely arrived!!!

Spelling Tip
Some words are easily confused because they have similar pronunciations and spellings. Check the signs to make sure that the words from the box are spelled correctly.

Word List
since	recent
sense	resent
choose	access
chose	excess
finally	later
finely	latter
except	metal
accept	medal
beside	personal
besides	personnel

Write Signs
On a separate piece of paper, create several signs that give helpful tips for employees, friends, family, or students. Try to use at least five of your spelling words.

© Scott Foresman 6

Notes for Home: Your child spelled words that are easily confused because they have similar pronunciations and spellings. **Home Activity:** Work with your child to design and decorate a poster that presents warnings or rules. Use some of the spelling words in your poster.

Spelling: Easily Confused Words   103

Name _____   Noah Writes a B & B Letter

Spelling: Easily Confused Words   REVIEW

Word List

since	finely	recent	latter
sense	except	resent	metal
choose	accept	access	medal
chose	beside	excess	personal
finally	besides	later	personnel

Directions: Choose the word from the box that contains each word below.
Write the word on the line.

1. ate _____
2. fine _____
3. sent _____
4. hose _____

5. cent _____
6. met _____
7. sides _____
8. sin _____

Directions: Choose a word from the box that best replaces the underlined
words in each book title. Write the word on the line.

_____ 9. <u>At Last</u>, We Were Champions!
_____ 10. Food Over Fashion: Who Cares About the <u>Second of the Two</u>?
_____ 11. Nothing Left to Say <u>but</u> Goodbye
_____ 12. A <u>Private</u> Memoir of My Life in Kenya
_____ 13. <u>Too Much</u> Is Never Enough for Some People
_____ 14. Ten Easy Steps to Popularity with Your <u>Employees</u>
_____ 15. Gold <u>Award</u> Champions of the Winter Olympics
_____ 16. How to Keep Your Pet <u>Next to</u> You When You Walk
_____ 17. Why No One Gets <u>Admittance</u> Without Proper I.D.
_____ 18. How To <u>Select</u> the Right Tile for Your Bathroom
_____ 19. Just Desserts: Sweets to Please Any <u>Awareness</u> of Taste
_____ 20. How to <u>Receive</u> a Compliment and What to Say Back

Notes for Home: Your child spelled words that are easily confused because they have similar pronunciations and spellings. **Home Activity:** Deliberately misuse some of the spelling words in sentences (for instance, use *sense* instead of *since*). Have your child correct the mistakes.

Name _____   Louis Braille

Spelling: Vowel Sounds /oi/, /ou/, /ȯ/

Pretest Directions: Fold back the page along the dotted line. On the blanks, write the spelling words as they are dictated. When you have finished the test, unfold the page and check your words.

1. _____
2. _____
3. _____
4. _____
5. _____
6. _____
7. _____
8. _____
9. _____
10. _____
11. _____
12. _____
13. _____
14. _____
15. _____
16. _____
17. _____
18. _____
19. _____
20. _____

1. He will **outlast** his opponent.
2. She opened a bank **account**.
3. The show will **astound** you.
4. A fence is an unnatural **boundary**.
5. The bird flew **southeast**.
6. Set the box on the **counter**.
7. The **sunflower** bloomed today.
8. We have to get there **somehow**.
9. I do not like this clam **chowder**.
10. That bully is really a **coward**.
11. The movie left us **disappointed**.
12. Their **voices** blended together.
13. They publish a weekly **tabloid**.
14. She is the **employee** of the year.
15. They gave a **joyful** shout.
16. The guests **applaud** the speaker.
17. Turn off that dripping **faucet**.
18. Proceed with **caution**.
19. She's my favorite **author**.
20. He was treated for mental **trauma**.

Pretest

Notes for Home: Your child took a pretest on words that have the vowel sounds /oi/, /ou/, and /ȯ/. **Home Activity:** Help your child learn misspelled words before the final test. Your child can underline the word parts that caused the problems and concentrate on those parts.

Spelling: Vowel Sounds /oi/, /ou/, /ȯ/   105

Name _____   Louis Braille

Spelling: Vowel Sounds /oi/, /ou/, /ȯ/

Think and Practice

Word List			
outlast	counter	disappointed	applaud
account	sunflower	voices	faucet
astound	somehow	tabloid	caution
boundary	chowder	employee	author
southeast	coward	joyful	trauma

Directions: Choose the words from the box with the vowel sound /ou/. Write each word in the correct column.

Words with /ou/ spelled ou

1. _____
2. _____
3. _____
4. _____
5. _____
6. _____

Words with /ou/ spelled ow

7. _____
8. _____
9. _____
10. _____

Directions: Choose the word from the box that best matches each clue. Write the word on the line.

_____ 11. I am a newspaper with huge headlines and lots of photos.

_____ 12. I work for another person.

_____ 13. I am how you feel when you don't achieve a goal.

_____ 14. I am a severe injury, wound, or shock.

_____ 15. We are what the singers in the choir use to make music.

_____ 16. I write books, plays, stories, and scripts.

_____ 17. I show concern for safety.

_____ 18. I am what you do when you clap your hands.

_____ 19. I am delighted and happy.

_____ 20. I am a fixture for drawing liquid from a pipe.

Notes for Home: Your child spelled words with the vowel sounds /oi/, /ou/, and /ȯ/. **Home Activity:** Challenge your child to spell words from the list in which *oy* spells the vowel sound in *boy* and *au* spells the vowel sound in *fault*.

106   Spelling: Vowel Sounds /oi/, /ou/, /ȯ/

Name _____   Louis Braille

Spelling: Vowel Sounds /oi/, /ou/, /ȯ/

Directions: Proofread this biography. Find seven spelling mistakes. Use the proofreading marks to correct each mistake.

≡	Make a capital.
/	Make a small letter.
∧	Add something.
⌒	Take out something.
⊙	Add a period.
¶	Begin a new paragraph.

Louis Braille lost his sight from a childhood trama, but he never felt limited by his blindness or any bowndry set by other people's thinking. More than one accownt of his life says that Braille got his idea for his system when he was only twelve. That is a fact sure to astouned anyone.

Braille worked for years to improve his idea until somehouw he invented the simple raised-dot system still in use today. Braille was disappoynted that his writing system was not officially recognized in his lifetime, but he would be joyful to learn that Braille writing is widely used now. It has managed to owtlast many other systems.

Spelling Tip
The vowel sound /ou/ is spelled **ou** and **ow**: **ou**tlast, someh**ow**. The vowel sound /oi/ is spelled **oi** and **oy**: v**oi**ces, j**oy**ful. The vowel sound /ȯ/ is often spelled **au**: **au**thor.

Write a Biography
Whom do you admire for his or her invention? On a separate sheet of paper, write a brief biography of the inventor of your choice. Explain why you feel his or her work is important. Try to use at least three spelling words.

Word List
outlast	disappointed
account	voices
astound	tabloid
boundary	employee
southeast	joyful
counter	applaud
sunflower	faucet
somehow	caution
chowder	author
coward	trauma

Notes for Home: Your child spelled words with the vowel sounds /oi/ spelled *oi* and *oy*, /ou/ spelled *ou* and *ow*, and /ȯ/ spelled *au*. **Home Activity:** Write the spelling words in a list. Include several misspellings. Invite your child to proofread and correct the list.

Name _____   Louis Braille

Spelling: Vowel Sounds
/oi/, /ou/, /ȯ/

REVIEW

Word List				
outlast	southeast	chowder	tabloid	faucet
account	counter	coward	employee	caution
astound	sunflower	disappointed	joyful	author
boundary	somehow	voices	applaud	trauma

Directions: Write the word from the box that belongs in each group.

1. worker, staff, _____
2. barrier, border, _____
3. someday, somewhere, _____
4. northeast, northwest, _____
5. happy, delighted, _____
6. care, wariness, _____
7. writer, journalist, _____

Directions: Choose the word from the box that best completes each sentence about a person's activity. Write the word on the line to the left.

_____ 8. The cook made _____ for the entire seafood restaurant.
_____ 9. The store clerk stood behind the _____ as he served the customers.
_____ 10. The magician was able to _____ the audience with his tricks.
_____ 11. The long-distance runner managed to _____ all her opponents in order to win.
_____ 12. The nurse monitored the patients in the _____ ward.
_____ 13. The audience stood to _____ the actor's fine performance.
_____ 14. The plumber tightened the bolt to fix the dripping _____.
_____ 15. The gardener was proud that his tall, yellow _____ won the contest.
_____ 16. The banker needed to fix the problems with an _____.
_____ 17. The _____ cringed with fear.
_____ 18. The reporter for the weekly _____ called in the story.
_____ 19. The singers' _____ sounded full, clear, and triumphant.
_____ 20. The manager was _____ when the shortstop made an error.

Notes for Home: Your child spelled words with the vowel sounds /oi/ spelled *oi* and *oy*, /ou/ spelled *ou* and *ow*, and /ȯ/ spelled *au*. **Home Activity:** Read a newspaper or magazine with your child. Make a list of other words that have these vowel sounds and spellings.

Name_____

The Librarian Who Measured the Earth

Spelling: Words from Greek and Latin

Pretest Directions: Fold back the page along the dotted line. On the blanks, write the spelling words as they are dictated. When you have finished the test, unfold the page and check your words.

1. _____
2. _____
3. _____
4. _____
5. _____
6. _____
7. _____
8. _____
9. _____
10. _____
11. _____
12. _____
13. _____
14. _____
15. _____
16. _____
17. _____
18. _____
19. _____
20. _____

1. Who invented the **automobile**?
2. He got the star's **autograph**.
3. The car has **automatic** windows.
4. She wrote her **autobiography**.
5. The plane was on **autopilot**.
6. This **telescope** is very powerful.
7. The speech will be **telecast** now.
8. He received an urgent **telegram**.
9. The **telegraph** wires fell down.
10. Is that the **telephone** ringing?
11. Her computer is **portable**.
12. We **import** toys into the country.
13. Cotton is an important **export**.
14. Trucks are used for **transport**.
15. He went to apply for a **passport**.
16. This is a sensitive **microphone**.
17. Please take off your **headphones**.
18. I play in a **symphony** orchestra.
19. He bought a new **saxophone**.
20. He sang into the **megaphone**.

Pretest

Notes for Home: Your child took a pretest on words with Greek and Latin word parts. *Home Activity:* Help your child learn misspelled words before the final test. Dictate the word and have your child spell the word aloud for you or write it on paper.

Spelling: Words from Greek and Latin **109**

Name _____

The Librarian Who Measured the Earth

Spelling: Words from Greek and Latin

Word List			
automobile	telescope	portable	microphone
autograph	telecast	import	headphones
automatic	telegram	export	symphony
autobiography	telegraph	transport	saxophone
autopilot	telephone	passport	megaphone

Directions: Choose the words from the box that have the Greek word part **auto-** and the Latin word part **phon**. Write each word in the correct column.

Words with auto-

1. _____
2. _____
3. _____
4. _____
5. _____

Words with phon

6. _____
7. _____
8. _____
9. _____
10. _____
11. _____

Directions: Use **port** or **tele-** to form a word from the box that completes each equation. Write the word on the line.

12. exact – act + ? = _____
13. microscope – micro + ? = _____
14. password – word + ? = _____
15. cablegram – cable + ? = _____
16. transform – form + ? = _____
17. phonograph – phono + ? = _____
18. remarkable – remark + ? = _____
19. forecast – fore + ? = _____
20. improve – prove + ? = _____

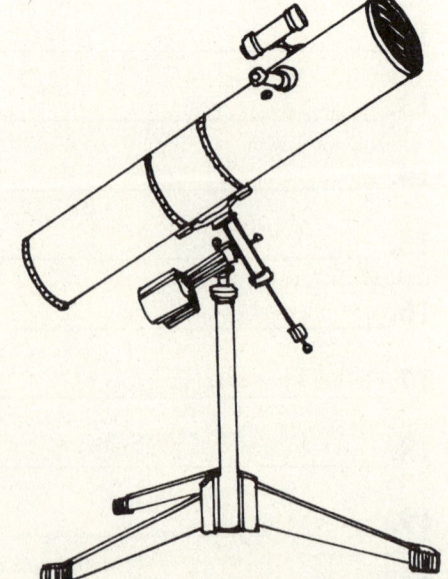

Notes for Home: Your child spelled words with Greek (*auto-, tele-*) and Latin (*port, phon*) word parts. *Home Activity:* Use the spelling words to create a set of word cards. Take turns choosing two cards to try to match words with the same Greek or Latin word parts.

Spelling: Words from Greek and Latin

Name _____

The Librarian Who Measured the Earth

Spelling: Words from Greek and Latin

Directions: Proofread this fact file. Find five spelling mistakes. Use the proofreading marks to correct each mistake.

≡ Make a capital.
/ Make a small letter.
∧ Add something.
⌴ Take out something.
⊙ Add a period.
¶ Begin a new paragraph.

Math in the Real World

1. Light bouncing off the moon into a telascope lens travels in a straight line.
2. A composer uses quarter notes, half notes, and other notes in a symphonie.
3. Some trucks can transport up to two tons of equipment.
4. If something gets between the signal and a portable telephone, the phone will not work properly.
5. The speed of an autimobile and how far it travels determines the time the trip will take.
6. Many computer programs have an auttomatic drawing tool for drawing shapes.

Spelling Tip
The Greek word part **tele-** means "far off." Be sure to keep the second **e** when spelling words with this word part. Remember, the word part has an **e** for each syllable: **t**e**l**e**phone.**

Word List

automobile	telescope	portable	microphone
autograph	telecast	import	headphones
automatic	telegram	export	symphony
autobiography	telegraph	transport	saxophone
autopilot	telephone	passport	megaphone

Write a Fact File

On a separate sheet of paper, create a fact file of your own. Give examples that show how mathematics or another school subject relates to everyday living. Try to use at least three spelling words.

Notes for Home: Your child spelled words with Greek *(auto-, tele-)* and Latin *(port, phon)* word parts. ***Home Activity:*** Give a clue that helps define each spelling word. Challenge your child to guess the word and spell it.

Spelling: Words from Greek and Latin

Name _____

The Librarian Who Measured the Earth

Spelling: Words from Greek and Latin

REVIEW

Word List				
automobile	autopilot	telegraph	export	headphones
autograph	telescope	telephone	transport	symphony
automatic	telecast	portable	passport	saxophone
autobiography	telegram	import	microphone	megaphone

Directions: Write the word from the box that belongs in each group.

1. oboe, clarinet, _____
2. binoculars, spyglass, _____
3. sonata, concerto, _____
4. vehicle, car, _____
5. memoir, life story, _____
6. move, carry, _____
7. message, wire, _____
8. pay phone, cell phone, _____
9. signature, name, _____
10. reflex, spontaneous, _____

Directions: Choose the word from the box that best completes each statement. Write the word on the line.

_____ 11. Retailer: "We should _____ more sweaters from Peru."

_____ 12. Director: "If I yell through the _____, they will all hear."

_____ 13. Pilot: "Let me adjust my _____ so I can hear the control tower."

_____ 14. Traveler: "My _____ shows that I am a Mexican citizen."

_____ 15. Producer: "The _____ of the World Series will air at 8:00."

_____ 16. Manufacturer: "We plan to _____ our products to China."

_____ 17. Astronaut: "If I set the shuttle's computer on _____, I can get some sleep."

_____ 18. Actor: "By using a _____, the back row will hear me, even if I'm speaking quietly."

_____ 19. Camper: "That small _____ stove is nice to have on a long hike."

_____ 20. Office Employee: "We used to _____ urgent messages."

Notes for Home: Your child spelled words with Greek (*auto-*, *tele-*) and Latin (*port*, *phon*) word parts. **Home Activity:** Work with your child to identify other words that have these same word parts.

112 Spelling: Words from Greek and Latin

Name _____ Tyree's Song

Spelling: Words with *ci* and *ti*

Pretest Directions: Fold back the page along the dotted line. On the blanks, write the spelling words as they are dictated. When you have finished the test, unfold the page and check your words.

1. _____
2. _____
3. _____
4. _____
5. _____
6. _____
7. _____
8. _____
9. _____
10. _____
11. _____
12. _____
13. _____
14. _____
15. _____
16. _____
17. _____
18. _____
19. _____
20. _____

1. Dogs are **social** creatures.
2. A diamond is a **precious** stone.
3. I never liked this **commercial**.
4. He is **especially** fond of berries.
5. The soda has **artificial** coloring.
6. Her aunt is a **financial** analyst.
7. Please thank our **gracious** hosts.
8. A **glacier** once covered the land.
9. What is our **national** bird?
10. Look it up in the **dictionary**.
11. The gears went into **motion**.
12. Which **position** do you play?
13. The **population** keeps growing.
14. Be **cautious** of strangers.
15. That is a very personal **question**.
16. I will consider your **suggestion**.
17. I forgot to **mention** my name.
18. He ate a **fraction** of the pie.
19. She collapsed from **exhaustion**.
20. Drinking liquids aids **digestion**.

Notes for Home: Your child took a pretest on words with the sound /sh/ spelled *ci* and *ti*. **Home Activity:** Help your child learn misspelled words. Have your child divide misspelled words into parts (such as syllables), concentrate on each part, and notice how the sound /sh/ is spelled.

Spelling: Words with *ci* and *ti*

Name _____   Tyree's Song

Spelling: Words with *ci* and *ti*

Word List

social	financial	motion	suggestion
precious	gracious	position	mention
commercial	glacier	population	fraction
especially	national	cautious	exhaustion
artificial	dictionary	question	digestion

Directions: Choose the words from the box that have the sound /**sh**/ spelled **ci** or **ti**. Write each word in the correct column. Hint: **ti** can also represent the sound /**ch**/.

/sh/ spelled ci

1. _____
2. _____
3. _____
4. _____
5. _____
6. _____
7. _____
8. _____

/sh/ spelled ti

9. _____
10. _____
11. _____
12. _____
13. _____
14. _____
15. _____
16. _____

Directions: Choose the word from the box that best matches each clue.

_____ 17. I am what you ask when you want to know the answer.

_____ 18. I am a condition of being extremely tired and worn out.

_____ 19. I am the process in your body that breaks down the food you eat.

_____ 20. I am what you offer when you have an opinion or recommendation.

Notes for Home: Your child spelled words with the sound /sh/ spelled *ci* and *ti* as in *espe**ci**ally* and *dic**ti**onary*, and the sound /ch/ spelled *ti* as in *ques**ti**on*. **Home Activity:** Help your child write humorous tongue-twister sentences that include several spelling words.

Name _____ Tyree's Song

Spelling: Words with *ci* and *ti*

Directions: Proofread these song lyrics. Find six spelling mistakes. Use the proofreading marks to correct each mistake.

The Martian Dilemma

≡ Make a capital.
/ Make a small letter.
∧ Add something.
⌒ Take out something.
⊙ Add a period.
¶ Begin a new paragraph.

Where has all the water gone—preshous water?

Is it in a glatier or an artifficial pool?

What can a population do with no water?

Be careful, don't be a fool!

Being cawtious is the rule.

Where will all the water go—that's the quesion.

Should we share our reservoirs, a nashional debate?

Let us learn new ways to find

Cool, clean water.

Spelling Tip
The sound /sh/ can be spelled *ci* or *ti*: **artifi*ci*al, na*ti*onal.** Check the song lyrics to make sure that words with this sound are spelled correctly.

Word List
social   motion
precious   position
commercial   population
especially   cautious
artificial   question
financial   suggestion
gracious   mention
glacier   fraction
national   exhaustion
dictionary   digestion

Write a Song
On a separate sheet of paper, write your own song lyrics. In your song, persuade others that your ideas about an issue are important. Try to use at least four spelling words.

Notes for Home: Your child spelled words with the sound /sh/ spelled *ci* and *ti* as in *especially* and *dictionary,* and the sound /ch/ spelled *ti* as in *question.* **Home Activity:** Say each spelling word twice. Have your child visualize each word and then spell it aloud.

Spelling: Words with *ci* and *ti* 115

Name _____ Tyree's Song

Spelling: Words with *ci* and *ti*   REVIEW

Word List

social	financial	motion	suggestion
precious	gracious	position	mention
commercial	glacier	population	fraction
especially	national	cautious	exhaustion
artificial	dictionary	question	digestion

Directions: Choose the word from the box that is the most opposite in meaning for each word below. Write the word on the line.

1. energy _____
2. whole _____
3. reckless _____
4. generally _____
5. answer _____
6. stillness _____
7. local _____
8. rude _____
9. natural _____
10. worthless _____

Directions: Choose a word from the box that best matches each definition. Write the word on the line.

_____ 11. a place or way of being placed
_____ 12. a hint, proposal, or recommendation
_____ 13. the process of breaking down food once eaten
_____ 14. an advertisement on television or on the radio
_____ 15. having to do with money
_____ 16. having to do with human beings and their relationships
_____ 17. a casual reference to something
_____ 18. the total number of people in a given area
_____ 19. a huge mass of ice
_____ 20. a book of words, origins, pronunciations, and definitions

Notes for Home: Your child spelled words with the sound /sh/ spelled *ci* and *ti* as in *especially* and *dictionary,* and the sound /ch/ spelled *ti* as in *question.* **Home Activity:** Scramble the letters of each spelling word. Challenge your child to unscramble them.

Name_____

Cutters, Carvers, and the Cathedral

Spelling: Related Words 2

Pretest Directions: Fold back the page along the dotted line. On the blanks, write the spelling words as they are dictated. When you have finished the test, unfold the page and check your words.

1._____	1. The road to my house is **direct**.
2._____	2. I went in the wrong **direction**.
3._____	3. He studied American **history**.
4._____	4. This is a **historical** site.
5._____	5. The **fact** is I am tired.
6._____	6. She gave a **factual** account.
7._____	7. He is a film **critic** on TV.
8._____	8. Don't **criticize** if you don't know.
9._____	9. The factories **produce** radios.
10._____	10. I help with the play's **production**.
11._____	11. He learned to do **magic** tricks.
12._____	12. The **magician** lost his wand.
13._____	13. He saw an **electric** eel.
14._____	14. The **electrician** fixed the lamp.
15._____	15. Their voices **distract** me.
16._____	16. That noise is a **distraction**.
17._____	17. What is a good cough **remedy**?
18._____	18. Her sister took **remedial** math.
19._____	19. Where is the **origin** of the stream?
20._____	20. This is an **original** story.

Notes for Home: Your child took a pretest on related words that have parts spelled similarly but pronounced differently. *Home Activity:* Help your child learn misspelled words before the final test by underlining the parts that are different in each pair and concentrating on those.

Spelling: Related Words 2   117

Name _____

Cutters, Carvers, and the Cathedral

Spelling: Related Words 2

Word List

direct	fact	produce	electric	remedy
direction	factual	production	electrician	remedial
history	critic	magic	distract	origin
historical	criticize	magician	distraction	original

Directions: Choose the pair of related words from the box that contain the same letter pronounced differently. Write the words in the correct group.

Word Pairs in Which the Sound of c is Different

1. _____   2. _____
3. _____   4. _____
5. _____   6. _____
7. _____   8. _____

Word Pairs in Which the Sound of t is Different

9. _____   10. _____
11. _____   12. _____
13. _____   14. _____

Directions: Choose the word in ( ) that best completes each sentence. Write the word on the line.

_____ 15. This arch is a (history/historical) monument that honors the war dead.

_____ 16. The monument has a long and colorful (history/historical).

_____ 17. The sculptor's (origin/original) idea had been for a statue, not an arch.

_____ 18. The marble used in the arch is of Italian (origin/original).

_____ 19. He needed a quick (remedy/remedial) when funding was cut back.

_____ 20. Fortunately, a millionaire gave some money as a (remedy/remedial) measure until further funds could be raised.

Notes for Home: Your child spelled related words that have parts with similar spellings but different pronunciations. *Home Activity:* Say each pair of related words aloud. Have your child spell each word and use it in a sentence.

118 Spelling: Related Words 2

Name _____

Cutters, Carvers, and the Cathedral

Spelling: Related Words 2

Directions: Proofread this passage from a gardening encyclopedia. Find five spelling mistakes. Use the proofreading marks to correct each mistake.

≡ Make a capital.
/ Make a small letter.
∧ Add something.
⌒ Take out something.
⊙ Add a period.
¶ Begin a new paragraph.

Landscape architects design parks and landscapes for the grounds around buildings. They are asked to produse pleasing and useful outdoor areas. Electric lights strung through tree branches look madgical when lit up at night. Highly originel and effective designs can remedee urban locations that are ugly and barren. Some gardens are designed strictly to focus attention on a beautiful view or the historrical features of a building. Whatever the project, landscape architects work magic with a combination of trees, shrubs, and flowers.

Spelling Tip
Related words often have parts that are spelled the same but that sound different: **direc_t_, direc_t_ion.** Check the passage to make sure that related words are spelled correctly.

Word List

direct	fact	produce	electric	remedy
direction	factual	production	electrician	remedial
history	critic	magic	distract	origin
historical	criticize	magician	distraction	original

Write an Article

Imagine that you are a writer of encyclopedias. On a separate sheet of paper, write an encyclopedia entry on some aspect of building, architecture, or construction. Describe the skills and training that are needed. Try to use at least three spelling words.

Notes for Home: Your child spelled related words that have parts with similar spellings but different pronunciations. **Home Activity:** Help your child write sentences that use pairs of related words. For example: *The historical society has a great interest in history.*

Spelling: Related Words 2   119

Name _____

Cutters, Carvers, and the Cathedral

Spelling: Related Words 2

REVIEW

Word List

direct	fact	produce	electric	remedy
direction	factual	production	electrician	remedial
history	critic	magic	distract	origin
historical	criticize	magician	distraction	original

Directions: Choose the word from the box that best matches each clue. Write the word on the line.

_____ 1. any point on the compass

_____ 2. a record of past events

_____ 3. a type of light that uses electricity

_____ 4. curing; relieving

_____ 5. source; starting point

_____ 6. statement that can be proven true or false

_____ 7. a person who makes judgments

_____ 8. concerned with history

_____ 9. the act or result of producing

_____ 10. something that makes it hard to concentrate

_____ 11. a type of trick, like pulling a rabbit out of a hat

_____ 12. to draw one's attention away from a task

_____ 13. a cure

Directions: Write the word from the box that belongs in each group.

14. authentic, unique, _____

15. clown, acrobat, _____

16. judge, analyze, _____

17. truthful, realistic, _____

18. plumber, engineer, _____

19. create, make, _____

20. order, command, _____

Notes for Home: Your child spelled related words that have parts with similar spellings but different pronunciations. *Home Activity:* Work with your child to create dictionary entries. For each spelling word, write a definition and an example sentence.

120 Spelling: Related Words 2